THE SILVERTOWN
EXPLOSION
LONDON 1917

THE SILVERTOWN EXPLOSION

LONDON 1917

Graham Hill & Howard Bloch

TEMPUS

First published 2003

Tempus Publishing Limited
The Mill, Brimscombe Port,
Stroud, Gloucestershire, GL5 2QG

British Library Cataloguing in Publication Data.
A catalogue record for this book is available from the British Library.

ISBN 0 7524 3053 X

Typesetting and origination by Tempus Publishing Limited
Printed in Great Britain by Midway Colour Print, Wiltshire

CONTENTS

Thanks to the Germanic Powers, who precipitated this orgy of blood out here, those of us who serve have become accustomed to sights of suffering and death on the battlefield, but it seems a hundred times more terrible when these things happen so far away from the shock of war, and involve so many helpless women and children.
(*Stratford Express*, 27 January 1917)

This book is dedicated to the memory of Howard Bloch (1955-2000), whose friendship and knowledge is sorely missed, and to my wife Carmel for her support and endless cups of coffee.

KEY TO MAP

1   Brunner Mond factory 'Danger Building', site of the explosion

2   Brunner Mond main factory

3   Silvertown Fire Station

4   Firemen's cottages

5   St Barnabas' Church

6   St Mark's Church

7   Vanesta Plywood Works

8   Silvertown Lubricant Works

9   Millennium Mills (set on fire by the explosion)

10 Premier Mills (also set on fire by the explosion)

This map has been compiled and reduced from the six-inch Essex (New Series) sheet LXXXVI, 14 and London sheet VI, 14 (1916). (Courtesy of Ordnance Survey)

INTRODUCTION

There was never any silver in Silvertown. Smoketown, Sulphurtown, the place could have been called any of those things and no one would have blinked.

Silvertown, M. Mcgrath

If you visit the Norman church of St Mary Magdalene at the bottom of High Street South in Newham and watch the traffic thundering along the busy A13 it is hard to imagine that the land between the road and the Thames was once marshland. In fact, until the mid-nineteenth century the whole area from the river to the line of the A13 and between Bow Creek and Barking Creek was uninhabited.

In the 1850s two events occurred which would shape the fabric of Silvertown for the next 150 years. One was the construction of the Royal Victoria Dock, opened in 1855 by Prince Albert. The other was the establishment of the S. W. Silver & Co. India rubber, gutta-percha and telegraph works, from which Silvertown gets its name. The Royal Albert Dock opened in 1880 and, with the Royal Victoria Docks, became the 'warehouse of the Empire'.

Soon other industries spread along the river and, with their insatiable demand for workers, whole streets of small houses soon sprung up jammed between the docks and factories. It was said that by the turn of the century every household in the country owned or had used at least one product that had come from Silvertown.

Jam, soap, chemicals, varnish, paint, boxes, oil and of course sugar from the large Tate & Lyle factory at Plaistow wharf were amongst the many items that came from this small, packed part of London. In the years leading up to the First World War, Silvertown, along with Canning Town and West Ham, had become the largest manufacturing centre in the south of England. However, by 1900 this rapid and uncontrolled development along with pollution from the many 'stink industries' led to countless health problems and insanitary conditions which encouraged the spread of diseases such as smallpox and cholera.

Brunner Mond's chemical works was established at the prime site of Crescent Wharf in West Silvertown in 1893. The main factory produced soda crystals while a second smaller plant manufactured caustic soda. The production of caustic soda was discontinued in 1912, and the plant was lying idle at the outbreak of the First World War.

When the First World War broke out in August 1914 there was great rejoicing, with the view that the Hun would be taught a lesson and that the boys would be home by Christmas. Sadly by Christmas the British army was stuck fast in the trenches of Flanders. The small army that had set out to such cheers was now being reinforced by Lord Kitchener's volunteers, whose numbers would soon be swelled by conscription. This huge increase in the Army, Navy and the new Royal Flying Corps led to a massive need for munitions that could not be fulfilled by existing suppliers. One particularly pressing need was that for high explosive shells. In order to increase production the Explosives Supply Department under Lord Moulton was set up. By May 1915 several new explosive factories had been opened but even these were not enough to keep up with demand. General Sir John French blamed British failure at the battle of Festubert in May 1915 on the shortage of high explosive shells. His views, later leaked to the press, were to cause the 'shell scandal' which contributed to the collapse of the Government. A new Ministry of Munitions under David Lloyd George was set up and the search for new sources of TNT redoubled. Lloyd George is quoted as saying: 'Even after utilising every workshop and factory capable of turning out munitions, we found that output would be inadequate unless we supplemented our resources by the setting up of emergency buildings' (*Silvertown 1917*).

TNT in its unrefined form was now becoming available in large quantities but it still needed purifying to make it suitable for use in high explosive shells and this led to a frantic search for the right type of factories. It was this search that led Lord Moulton to the idle Brunner Mond works at Crescent Wharf, Silvertown. It was understood from the start that locating a TNT factory in the heart of such a densely populated area was 'very dangerous' but such was the need that it was felt by the Ministry of Munitions to be 'worth the risk'. Dr F.A. Freeth, Brunner Mond's chief chemist in 1917, is quoted as saying:

> Our managing director said: 'Why should we not use the vacuum plant at Silvertown for this process?' It worked, but was manifestly very dangerous. At the end of every month we used to write to Silvertown to say that their plant would go up sooner or later, and we were told that it was worth the risk to get the TNT. One day it did go up, with well-known results.
>
> (Dr F.A. Freeth, *New Scientist* 30 July 1964)

The factory was ideal as all that was required was the addition of a melt pot at the smaller caustic soda plant to make it ready for its new use as a 'danger building'. Unfortunately this 'danger building' would only be some 200 yards from the dense rows of workers' houses and right in the middle other factories and wharves containing flour, oil, varnish, wood, chemicals and many other highly combustible materials. In September 1915 the plant began production. However, as Brunner Mond's own history states, 'the demand soon overtook the capacity of the plant, which never exceeded about nine tons per day ... and Lord Moulton then asked the Company to build new works for TNT purification.' In February

1916 the new TNT factory was opened by Brunner Mond on a plot of land in the township of Rudheath, Cheshire, about one mile from Northwich station. Even though the factory was a vast improvement both in terms of production and safety, Silvertown was not shut down.

The process undertaken at the Silvertown plant was TNT purification. Crude TNT arrived at the works in sacks or wooden barrels. The crude material was unpacked and loaded by hand into a large melting pot heated by steam coils. Molten TNT was then run off into dissolvers, containing alcohol, where it was then stirred in a partial vacuum to crystallise it. The cooled TNT was then spun in centrifuges to remove impurities. This process was then repeated in a separate melting pot to further purify the TNT after which it was run into a pan where a water cooled roller caused it to solidify. It was then scraped off the coolers with a blade to form 'flake TNT' which was collected into cotton bags for despatch.

The main factory employed 268 workers, and 63 worked in the 'danger building' in three shifts of 21 to ensure continuous production with Dr Lamb in charge. Dr Andrea Angel was brought in as chief chemist at £400 per year.

The danger became a reality at 6.52 p.m. on Friday 19 January 1917 when a fire in the melt-pot room caused about 50 tons of TNT to explode and turned Brunner Mond's into a bomb. Buildings in the immediate vicinity, including Vanesta's plywood factory and the oil tanks at Silvertown Lubricants, caught fire; the fire station opposite and several streets of small houses were demolished; fires raged in the flour mills in the Royal Victoria Dock; and many other buildings, including St Barnabas' Church and its hall, were badly damaged.

People all over London heard the explosion and felt the blast, which damaged between 60,000 and 70,000 properties, and saw a red glow in the sky that was visible for miles around. Considering the force of the explosion and the nature of the district, casualties were remarkably few. Seventy-three people were killed and several hundred injured. West Ham Council and a large number of local and national organisations were soon on the scene providing practical assistance for the injured and those who had been made homeless. The Government held an inquiry into the cause of the explosion which was widely rumoured to have been caused by a German agent.

The first report appeared in *The Times* of Monday 22 January 1917:

MUNITIONS FACTORY EXPLOSION,

ACCIDENT NEAR LONDON,

CONSIDERABLE LOSS OF LIFE.

The following official statement was issued by the Ministry of Munitions late last night:- The Minister of Munitions regrets to announce that an explosion occurred this evening at a munitions factory in the neighbourhood of London. It is feared that the explosion was attended by considerable loss of life and damage to property.

A fuller report followed on Monday 22 January:

The great explosion ... on Friday night proves to have been less destructive of human life than was first feared.... The total number of deaths was about a hundred and the injured may perhaps number four hundred.

A Government Inquiry was set up and it reported its findings on 23 January. The report, which is reproduced in full in this book, did not identify a clear cause for the disaster but came to the conclusion that the fire which led to the explosion was caused by 'a detonation spark produced by friction or impact', or 'spontaneous ignition of the TNT in or about the melt pot'. Sabotage was not ruled out, as 'in the circumstances and for the reasons given in this report the possibility of the disaster having been maliciously caused cannot be disregarded.... In the course of our investigations a very unsatisfactory state of affairs has been disclosed regarding the condition in which the packages of TNT arrived at Rainham on their way to Silvertown. In many cases, the heads of barrels and kegs were driven in or missing and the calico bags containing the TNT exposed. In some instances the bags themselves were torn. This condition of things constitutes a serious danger both from the point of view of accident and as affording opportunity for malicious tampering with the TNT. The report clearly raises very grave questions so far as the Ministry is concerned and makes serious reflections on the supply Department.'

The report also criticised Brunner Mond for the practice of purifying and storing TNT in the same building, and states that

> It is an axiom of explosives technology that the risk of disaster in a working building is never absent, whereas an accident in connection with the mere storing of explosives is a extremely rare occurrence.... The existence of magazines would have enabled the amount of material in the working building to have been reduced to the minimum necessary for the process.... If this consideration had been acted upon at Silvertown, and the bulk of the TNT had been kept in buildings separate from the plant, a disaster of this magnitude might have been avoided.

The official figures given at the Inquiry were '69 killed on the spot, 98 were seriously injured, of which 4 have since died in hospital, and 328 slightly injured. In addition we are informed by the police that between 500 and 600 persons who received cuts and bruises were treated in the street or by private practitioners.'

The scale of the damage to local industry can be shown by the claims submitted for damages to the Ministry of Munitions.

Port of London Authority	£357,540
Vanesta Ltd	£338,515
Vernon & Sons	£300,141
Silvertown Lubricants Ltd	£102,250
British Alizarine Co Ltd	£41,193
John Knight Ltd	£38,000
A. Lyle & Sons Ltd	£39,060

Richard Moreland & Son Ltd	£33,230
Spencer, Chapman & Messel Ltd	£30,761
South Metropolitan Gas Co.	£20,000
Silvertown Manure Works	£15,332
Payments put aside for smaller companies	£169,500

(*East End Then and Now*)

The explosion was widely covered in the national and local press, but these accounts were subject to censorship. As other events occurred, coverage in the press gradually diminished.

The Silvertown Explosion holds the record of being the largest single explosion in London and local reminders of this tragic incident still surface today:

From the mid 1960s to the end of the 1980s I worked in a factory adjacent to the Brunner Mond site, and at that time little was known or spoken about the actual incident. I had often wondered why, in a very crowded area, there was a huge unbuilt, open site used only for parking large vehicles, and when I asked, older employees told me that they had heard that an explosion had happened there during World War One and that no one wanted to build there. That was all I knew until a 'company' magazine published an article to commemorate the event's seventy-fifth anniversary.

(Lal Cook)

Notes on the articles

This publication brings together for the first time a diverse range of primary sources including first-hand accounts and reports including the Government report on the explosion which is reproduced in full, courtesy of the Public Record Office at Kew. The conclusions of this report note the failure to identify the cause of the fire that led to the explosion, but make some striking recommendations, including the repeal of a clause that exempted TNT from inclusion in the Explosives Act of 1910. Many of the following articles had a limited circulation and would generally not have been available to a wider readership. For example, the *Essex Volunteer Regiment Magazine* was produced for members of that unit and contains detailed information about its work after the explosion. Copies of most of these small-circulation publications are held in Newham Archives and Local Studies Library.

The reports of the explosion and its aftermath make clear the extent of the devastation, the practical work undertaken and the difficulties faced by the various organisations that were familiar with the poor social conditions prevailing in the area. West Ham Council, through its Emergency Committee and Silvertown Explosion Committee, was able to co-ordinate the efforts of the groups and organisations involved, and also played a vital role in the welfare of those made homeless.

In addition, there are first-hand accounts by Fireman J.J. Betts who served at Silvertown fire station, a worker at St Barnabas' Church and the Revd G. Mitchell, Chaplain in the Port of London. These give graphic descriptions of how the dramatic events of 19 January 1917 affected their lives.

The official number of those killed by the explosion is the same as the number listed by the *Stratford Express*. However, research in *The Times* and other sources have brought additional names to light. The newspaper reported on many aspects of the explosion from survivor's accounts to council meetings and the inquest itself. The reports stress the gallantry of the firemen, policemen and other organisations involved with the tragedy and they also include the many messages of sympathy that were sent to the area. The funerals are also covered in some detail and reports on these show the very real sense of grief and mourning felt by the community itself and the country in general.

There are a number of reports on the work of West Ham Council and its response to the explosion. A significant feature of these is that there is virtually no criticism on the siting of a high explosive factory in such a densely populated area. Indeed, the only notes of dissension came from the Independent Labour Party and the Dock, Wharf, Riverside and General Workers' Union.

The *Stratford Express* reports are taken directly from editions dated 27 January, 3 February and 10 February 1917. The newspaper was published twice a week, on Wednesday and Saturday, with reports repeated in each edition. Although the explosion occurred on Friday 19 January, it was not reported in the newspaper until Wednesday 24. As the Saturday editions reprinted Wednesday's reports and included extra articles and a full editorial, only the Saturday editions are included.

Newspapers printed during wartime are often subject to censorship and the *Stratford Express* was no exception. Therefore Brunner Mond's is referred to throughout the text as 'a munitions factory' and Silvertown is 'the affected district'. A rare exception is where in one paragraph reference is made to the 'Mayor of West Ham'. Also no churches or schools are named and where it has been possible to identify them, their names have been included as a footnote. These are the only additions to the original text and we have included mis-spellings of names where they occur. For instance, in the first edition Dr Angel is spelt Dr Angell and Mr Wainwright's first name Geoffrey is also printed as Jeffrey. The most common spelling of the names of those killed in the explosion is included in the list of casualties at the end of this publication.

CHAPTER I
COUNTY BOROUGH OF
WEST HAM FIRE BRIGADE

In an official report issued two days after the disastrous explosion at Silvertown mention is made of the destruction of a fire-engine and the miraculous escape of several firemen. One of these was the author of this chapter, Mr J.J. Betts, of the Silvertown Fire Station.

This extract is taken from The Great War *Part 33, 243 'I Was There'.*

When Death Came to Silvertown
I Saw the Worst War-Time Explosion
by Ex-Fireman J.J. Betts

It was ten minutes to seven; a chilly starry night on January 19, 1917. The war had dragged on for two and half years. I was on night duty with a number of others of the brigade at Silvertown Fire Station in Poplar, E.

On every side loomed the black shapes of factories. Behind screened windows – for every precaution was taken in those days of air raids, and not a light showed – vast armies of war workers were engaged on their various tasks of turning out munitions, food, and clothing for the troops.

Opposite the fire station was the munitions factory of Messrs. Brunner Mond, Limited. Behind it were the flour mills of W. Vernon & Sons. A little to the east were the oil refineries of Silvertown Lubricants Limited, and the saw-mill and creosote works of Messrs. Burt, Boulton & Haywood. To the west stretched the sugar factory of Messrs. Lyle Limited.

Nearly 5,000 workers were there in all – hundreds of them women and girls who were 'doing their bit' in the absence at the front of husbands, fathers, sons and sweethearts.

Perhaps the most important of these factories was that of Messrs. Brunner Mond, for it was here that night and day, the ceaseless task of manufacturing shells and armaments was taking place. The hourly cry from the front was 'More munitions.'

Not the least important branch of the vital work of munition making was carried out in the chemical laboratories which lay a little away from the main works. These were the 'danger buildings', where high explosives were manufactured.

From all sides came the din of racing machinery, the mournful whine of sawmills, and the rattle of cranes as barges lying in the Thames were loaded.

Pedestrians hurried past the fire station to and from their work, for it was about the hour when shifts were changed. Children, carrying baskets of provisions and enamel tea-cans, the evening meals of parents working overtime, hastened on their way. There was in the air the electrical tension brought about by high speed production in an urgent cause.

Suddenly, without warning, a bright orange tongue of flame shot up from the very heart of the Brunner Mond works high into the air, all the more vivid on account of the enveloping blackness of the night. Into the station rushed one of the men. 'Brunner Mond's alight!' he shouted.

None knew better than we the terrible implications conveyed by that brief warning. For if one those rising flames reached the danger buildings, there was little hope for the lives and property in the vicinity. There was, too, a further danger, for besides the vast quantity of T.N.T. contained in the 'danger' building, there lay on the permanent way that ran close to the building four railway trucks containing enough of the deadly stuff to blow up half London.

Within a few seconds fire alarms rang through the station, and our chief immediately rapped out orders. We rushed to get out the escape and the pump. There was not a second to lose if we were to quell the fire and avert an explosion. But I felt it was such a forlorn hope that I yelled to my wife, who, with our twelve-year-old son, lived in the quarters behind the station: 'Get out of it, Polly, for God's sake! We're all going up in a minute!' The next second we were tearing across the road into Brunner Mond's yard.

Outside the fire station people stood transfixed as though fascinated by that now fiercely burning building across the way. Others were fleeing helter-skelter anyhow – anywhere from that flaring presage of the imminent danger, yelling warnings as they went. Some lay flat on their faces on the pavement, some prayed against walls of the street.

As we entered the factory gates we were met by the flying figure of the timekeeper, a burly Scotsman. 'Run for it, mon, we'll be gone in a minute!' he yelled to me as he almost staggered, past, hatless, distraught, his face distorted by a terrible fear. They were his last words.

Then it was as though heaven had giddily plunged to meet the earth in a shattering upheaval. In one second the whole world seemed to have crumbled.

It might have been seconds, minutes, hours, before I next remembered. I was lying on my back on a piece of waste ground 200 feet from the spot where I and other firemen had been fixing the hose ready to play on the flames.

Around me was a vast plain of rubble. The factory had gone. There was fearful sounds in the air, the screams of injured women and children, the groans of those imprisoned under the debris, the rattle of rafters and girders being feverishly overturned by rescuers who had rushed to the shattered area, the shrill resonance of ambulance bells, the imperious clang of fire alarms, the roar of flames.

On every side great fires were blazing. In all nine factories and mills had caught alight, ignited by red-hot iron girders, flung skyhigh by the explosion, falling into their midst.

Something of the terrific force of the explosion can be imagined when I tell you that parts of our fire-engine was found a quarter of a mile away, smashed and twisted almost beyond recognition. Enormous boilers were hurled into the air and landed several streets away. Houses were left with cracking walls, windows gone, doors blown in, and roofs with gaping holes. In places which received the full force of the explosion it was as though a giant pestle had descended from the heavens and pounded them to powder.

Every building in London was shaken. Half a million windows in shops and houses across the river a mile away at Charlton and South Woolwich were broken. The explosion was heard in districts as far apart as Salisbury and King's Lynn.

Meanwhile the surrounding factories burned fiercely, and the task of rescuing workers in their blazing depths began. Every available fire-engine and escape from all parts of London converged on Silvertown. It was a grim and awe-inspiring scene. For three or four hours after the explosion the whole of London was lit by the flames.

The fire area itself was an astonishing spectacle. Imagine an arc of towering flat-faced factories, with many rows of windows. At that moment they were as if they had been filled with burning coal. Every window opening glared like an iron furnace when the doors are opened.

Through long cracks in the walls long flames waved out like fiery serpents. Now a great fragment of iron – it looked as large as a cottage roof – would slide down the sides of the gleaming pile. Towards the river another great factory blazed fiercely. Its windows appeared like a series of white-hot ingots. To the right the widespread frame of a row of timber sheds resembled a great main line railway station afire.

The scene seemed unreal.

There were these towering bonfires of light spread out across the black landscape, and as their flames leaped up into the sky they threw into relief the broken shells of rows of houses – streets without windows, and, what was more, without inhabitants.

Some were dead – no one knew yet how many. The rest were gone – anywhere away from the scene of death and destruction.

High overhead poured vast clouds of smoke. Beneath them from the flour mills, where several hundred girls had been at work, came flying showers of millions of tiny particles of light as though a sweeping storm of sleet had become incandescent. No doubt these tiny specks were the glowing ashes of a myriad grains of wheat carried up into the sky by the waves of flame. It was like a golden rainstorm. The firemen and their apparatus were almost helpless against conflagrations of such number and magnitude.

For days afterwards the heaps of debris in the midst of the mere shells of these mills and factories that remained were smouldering. Weeks afterwards when the task of clearing away the wreckage began, the workers came across red-hot embers deep down among the pile of debris.

While the great battle against the fires was being waged by firemen, a large army of helpers was helping to extricate the dead and injured from the wreckage of the homes. The heaps of ruins which had been houses were slowly explored. It was like scraping and scratching among great rubbish heaps. Sometimes a distracted mother in search of a missing child would push to the forefront of a group of searchers and herself claw at the pile of rubble in a frenzy of apprehension, until her fingers bled. Such scenes were frequent.

One of the bodies dug out was that of a young clerk engaged in the sugar refinery, one of the factories set ablaze. This youth had run from the factory to a manager's house close by to warn him of the fire. As he was knocking at the door the explosion occurred, and the wall of the house collapsed and buried him.

One woman was putting her babies to bed when the explosion occurred. She rushed out with them, and in her terror ran on till she was taken in by some kindly people, at whose house she stayed. A number became mentally unhinged by the shock. My wife was rendered stone deaf.

One encountered at every turn stories of simple heroism and human fortitude in the face of terrible calamity. There were tales of rescues by those who themselves were seriously injured. One man dragged four badly injured young children from the wreckage of a demolished house, and it was not until afterwards, when he suddenly sank into unconsciousness, that those around realized that he had himself lost a foot.

There was one brave girl, Norah Griffiths, who helped to hold up a roof that would otherwise have fallen and crushed to death a number of young children attending a Band of Hope meeting at a local mission hall.

People divested themselves of their outer garments, despite the bitterly cold weather, in order to wrap up the shivering forms of homeless children, scores of whom had been separated from their parents in the darkness and confusion.

In every street stood groups of stranded people, gazing ruefully at what had once been their homes. In many cases the roofs and the bedrooms had just disappeared. Only parts of the walls of the downstairs rooms were left. These rooms were no longer rooms. They had no ceilings; their fronts had vanished. One of the most immediate and pressing problems was the housing of the homeless. The Salvation Army did wonderful work. It established shelters in every available building, and provided food and hot drinks. A nearby chapel was hastily converted into a crèche, and hundreds of children there found shelter. Some of the victims sought refuge farther afield, at the houses of relatives, at charitable institutions. With the coming of dawn there were still hundreds of homeless ones, weary and pale-faced, trudging the dismal streets.

The entire district was cut off by a military guard and police forces, and through this cordon passed a stream of refugees from the stricken area in search of food and sleep. Some clutched the glass vases which had adorned their mantelpieces, for in many cases it seemed to have been the most fragile articles that had escaped injury. Others carried clothes-baskets filled with personal trifles salved from the ruins of their homes. Everyone seemed to bear a load of some sort – trunks, sacks, bundles, even treasures hastily wrapped in sheets and blankets.

Some wheeled perambulators loaded with household goods. There were baths filled with bedding and clothes recovered from the wreckage. And hundreds who had fled from the place as soon as they had overcome the great shock of the explosion, and had begged a night's lodging a few miles away, tramped back to see what they could salvage from the wreckage of their former homes.

How little the world at large knew of this and a score of other similar war-time disasters involving loss of life and injury among the civilian population!

Seventy-four lives had been lost, nearly a thousand maimed and injured. The place which had been a munitions works was a waste of black desolation. Nearly a dozen factories and mills had been destroyed. Thousands of houses were wiped out. Hundreds of people were rendered homeless. The damage amounted to £1,212,661. There were third-party claims running into several million pounds sterling.

A dozen people living in the immediate vicinity of the explosion were never seen again.

This terrible story of death and destruction was told to the world the next morning in the following prosaic announcement which appeared in the daily newspapers:

The Ministry of Munitions regret to announce that an explosion occurred this evening at a munitions factory in the neighbourhood of London.

It is feared that the explosion was attended by considerable loss of life and damage to property.

That is war.

CHAPTER 2
BRUNNER MOND & CO.

Note: this comes from Brunner Mond's own 'in-house' publication of 1923.

The First Fifty Years of Brunner Mond & Co. 1873–1923

T.N.T.

In addition to the urgent demand for ammonium nitrate, there arose an outcry for trinitrotoluene (T.N.T.) for filling shells, and Lord Moulton immediately set to work to satisfy it. Not only had he to secure the supplies of toluene, but he had also to urge manufacturers to provide concentrated sulphuric acid and nitric acid. When he had made sure that T.N.T. could be obtained in quantity, there still remained the problem of how to purify it to render it suitable for filling shells. He came to Brunner, Mond & Co. to ask for help and, learning that the works at Silvertown, where the manufacture of caustic soda had been discontinued in 1912, were standing idle, he pressed for their transformation to work a process that consisted of melting the crude TNT in hot methylated spirit, and then cooling it to free it from impurities. The Company strongly expressed their reluctance to carry on such a dangerous manufacture in a densely populated district; but the urgency was so great that they eventually consented.

The works were quickly transformed, and started in September, 1915. The process proved satisfactory so far as the product was concerned, but it was laborious on account of the large volume of spirit that had to be distilled, and the demand soon overtook the capacity of the plant, which never exceeded about nine tons per day. Lord Moulton then asked the Company to build new works for T.N.T. purification, and accepted their suggested new process, which effected the purification by grinding the crude material in a mill flooded with warm alcohol, filtering the mixture and then melting the T.N.T. ready for solidification on a flaking machine. The Company offered a plot of land in the township of Rudheath, about one mile from Northwich Station, and rapidly built works there, the first unit being put in operation within a few months (in February, 1916). From the name of the stream that flowed through the land, they were christened the 'Gadbrook Works.' In face of an ever-increasing demand, unit after unit was added, and extensions were added and were carried out up to the end of the war. The output of purified T.N.T. eventually reached nearly sixty tons per day.

The situation of these works had been very carefully chosen, and with the exception of one farm building there was not an inhabited house within half a mile. On account of the extreme liability of T.N.T. to take fire, water tanks were placed in each unit, and pipes were so arranged that any part of the plant could be drenched in an instant. It was recognised that in an atmosphere always charged with the vapour of alcohol a fire once started might spread with alarming rapidity. On one or two occasions fire did occur, but it was immediately extinguished by flooding with water. On one day, however, there was cause for grave anxiety, because while rodding through the choked outlet of a vessel, the T.N.T. took fire under water and burned until it was all decomposed, in spite of the fact that numerous hosepipes from the fire engines were discharging water through it all the time. In recognition of their bravery upon this occasion, resulting in the probable saving of life, the King awarded Leonard Harper the Albert Medal, and made W.R. Storey a member of the Order of the British Empire.

It is much to be regretted that when Gadbrook Works were started the Silvertown plant was not stopped, because its situation was never suitable for the handling of high explosive, and the only reason for ever starting the manufacture there was the existence of idle plant which could be adapted in a short space of time. Unfortunately, in January, 1917, while a number of men, led by Andrea Angel (an Oxford don who had volunteered for war work) were trying to quell a fire in the plant, a disastrous explosion destroyed not only the whole works but also a large number of dwelling-houses in the vicinity. Angel, fourteen men, and one woman were killed by the explosion. For his valiant attempt to save life, the King made a posthumous award of the Edward Medal to Angel.

CHAPTER 3
REPORT OF THE SILVERTOWN EXPLOSION COMMITTEE

Note: On Saturday 20th January, Alderman R. Mansfield, Mayor of West Ham, called an emergency meeting at Lees Hall Barking Road at which the Silvertown Explosion Committee was formed. The Committee met daily to oversee the rehousing of those made homeless and the rebuilding and repair of the many damaged houses The reports were published in the council's minutes (West Ham Council Committee Reports, Volume 31b, Chapter 3, 1917).

County Borough of West Ham
Report of the Silvertown Explosion Committee

The disastrous explosion at Silvertown on the 19th January, 1917, rendered practically homeless the residents in the West Silvertown area, and a large number of the unfortunate sufferers were sheltered and cared for in the Lees Hall, Barking Road, various Institutions, and by private individuals, during the night. On the following day this accommodation was found to be quite inadequate, and it became necessary to at once institute an organisation to arrange for the housing and feeding of the increasing numbers needing assistance. With this object, the Explosion Emergency Committee was formed, with the Mayor (Alderman R. Mansfield, J.P.) as Chairman, and Miss Towers and Mr. J.J. Harding as Hon. Secretaries. Centres were opened at:-

The Baptist Tabernacle, Barking Road

Canning Town Congregational School, Swanscombe Street

Cory Institute (Canning Town Wesleyan Church)

Mansfield House Boys' Club (Fairbairn Hall)

St. Margaret's (Roman Catholic) School

Mary Street Primitive Methodist Church

St. Matthew's, Custom House

St. Gabriel's Church, Canning Town, and

Hermit Road Council School

and thanks to the good work done all who were, for the time being, homeless were promptly provided for.

At the meeting of the Council on the 23rd January, 1917, the Mayor referred to the assistance and help which had been rendered to the homeless, and the accommodation provided by the different organisations and Churches in the Southern portion of the Borough and expressed his high appreciation of, and deep thanks for all that had been done on behalf of the sufferers, whilst the Council accorded their very best thanks to the members of the Emergency Committee for the splendid work which they had done and to all those who had in any way assisted in the relief work.

At that meeting a letter was read stating that the Local Government Board had been requested by the Prime Minister and the Minister of Munitions to undertake, in co-operation with the Local Authorities, the provision of temporary assistance for the suf-ferers, and to supervise the application of any funds available for the purpose, and suggesting that the Council should appoint a Special Committee of their own members, with other persons representa-tive of the various interests concerned, which would be responsible for the administration of any funds placed at their disposal, by the Board.

The Committee was constituted as follows:-

The Mayor,

Aldermen Davis and White,

Councillors Croot, Filmer, Flaxman, Godbold, Gray, Holland, Hollins, Jones, Kensett and Wordley.

The Council expressed the unanimous wish that the Special Committee should work in conjunction with the Emergency Committee, and the latter were invited to continue the good work they had already done. To further this object the Emergency Committee, at the request of the Special Committee, appointed the Rev. R.R. Clifford, the Rev. F.W. Blackwell and Mr. N.M. Hyde, with the Hon. Secretaries, to serve on the latter Committee and the experience which these members brought to the Committee proved exceedingly helpful.

One of the first duties of the Committee was to agree the scale of temporary assistance to be afforded to the sufferers, and a deputation consisting of the Mayor and Councillors Hollins, Jones, and Wordley waited on the Local Government Board, with the result that the Board fixed the following scale:-

		£	s.	d.
Adult		0	16	0
do.	and 1 child	1	3	0
do.	and 2 children	1	8	0
do.	and 3 do.	1	11	6
do.	and 4 do.	1	14	6
do.	and 5 do.	1	17	6
do.	and 6 do.	2	0	6
do.	and 7 do.	2	3	6

Plus 3s for each additional child.

All over 16 years of age were treated as adults, and the amount of 16s. was paid in respect of each adult.

An office for the payment of funds to assist the sufferers was opened at the Public Hall, Canning Town, on the 26th January, and remained open for ten days. When the large number of persons who were in need of temporary help only were disposed of the office was opened in the morning alone for such time as was found needful. This period covered two weeks, and dealt generally with people whose livelihood were suspended by reason of the destruction of the premises in which they pursued their vocations. The remaining class for whom the office was opened twice weekly, Wednesday and Saturday, consisted mostly of those injured or the dependents of workers who were casualties in the Explosion. The office was last opened on the 17th March, and thereafter the persons (at that date 42) needing relief were visited in their homes by two members of the Staff who made the authorised payments and incidentally satisfied themselves that the relief was necessary and proper. This list gradually reduced in numbers as the Ministry settled the claims of the recipients and a few only continued to be paid up to 11th August.

The Town Clerk's Staff on whom the allocation and dispersal of the monies rested were assisted in the early days when the work was heaviest by several gentlemen who were teachers in the Schools damaged by the Explosion, and their assistance willingly given enabled the large volume of work involved to be carried out with the smallest delay to the unfortunate people whose necessities attempts were made to quickly meet. A member of the Staff of the Borough Treasurer made the actual payments, and his assistance was most cheerfully given.

During the early days the members of the Relief Sub-Committee were in constant attendance and gave instructions in cases of difficulty or doubt, so that all claims were promptly dealt with.

The Local Government Board also sanctioned the payment of reasonable Funeral Expenses not exceeding £9 in each case, and arrangements were also made in conjunction with the Ministry of Munitions for immediate payments not exceeding £10, or in special cases not exceeding £20, for the replacement of essential furniture destroyed in whole or part as a result of the Explosion.

These claims for essential furniture were investigated and paid out by members of the Town Clerk staff, but principally by Mr. E. O. Weddell, who devoted his entire time to this work as well as to the payments to the sufferers at their homes, and although not in robust health he did not spare himself in his endeavours to carry out with commendable celerity and sympathy the duties which were required of him.

The work of caring and providing for those remaining in the temporary shelters was continued by the Superintendents in charge, and the Committee owe them a deep debt of gratitude for their services and also the body of able and sympathetic workers who rallied round them. No praise is too high for the admirable manner in which this difficult and arduous task was carried through. Thanks are also due to the National Food Supply who sent down food to the value of £300.

The Committee in this connection record their gratitude to the West Ham Board of Guardians, the Whitechapel and Poplar Guardians and the Red Cross Society for the loan of blankets and bedding at very short notice, and to the Women's Reserve Ambulance and others who lent motor vehicles for transport purposes.

The first few days after the Explosion were devoted to the removal of furniture from the wrecked homes, the Ministry of Munitions placing several lorries at the disposal of the Committee. Most valuable voluntary services were rendered by the Salvation Army, the Church Army, and by many of the local contractors, among whom should be mentioned Messrs. E. & A. Shadrack, Thos. Feast Ltd., Mr. J. Benton, Anglo-American Oil Co., Mr. J. Welch, Messrs. Keiller & Son, Ltd., Messrs. R. Moreland & Son Ltd., and the East Anglian Coal Co., some of whom also provided storage facilities; as did the West Ham Board of Guardians and the Manager of the Council's Stable Department.

This work was rendered more difficult on account of the very cold weather prevailing and of the dearth of houses to which the people could be removed.

Valuable help not only in the removal of furniture, but in providing an ambulance party at Lees Hall, and guards at Hermit Road School and other centres was given by the lst Battn. Essex Volunteer Regt., Ambulance Sergt. E.J. May being released from his scholastic duties by the Chairman of the Education Committee in order to enable him to devote his whole time to this work.

Adequate funds were from time to time placed at the disposal of the Committee by the Local Government Board, thus rendering an appeal to the public unnecessary but notwithstanding this contributions to a considerable amount came unsolicited to the Mayor from all parts of the country, and in some cases from the Colonies.

Many gifts of clothing were also received, which were distributed by the Emergency Committee, and proved of great value in the hour of need. The generous thanks of the Committee are heartily accorded to all those who assisted in this way.

The work of restoring the damaged houses was promptly undertaken by H.M. Office of Works, and large bodies of men were busily engaged with the object of getting the people re-housed in the shortest possible time. Very commendable progress was made, and the efforts of Mr. Watts Johnson, the Resident Superintendent, to procure an early completion of the work met with great success.

Apart altogether from the policy of restoring the houses instead of clearing the area and re-erecting dwellings on a more up-to-date plan, it cannot be denied that the houses in their restored condition are a great improvement on the old state of affairs, both as regards stability and sanitary conditions, and the thanks of the Committee are due to the Office of Works for the expeditious and satisfactory manner in which the job was carried through. It is no exaggeration to say that the Government's action in undertaking the work, instead of relying upon the property owners led to a great saving in time, and as events proved, the only possible solution of a difficult situation.

One of the hardest tasks imposed upon the Committee was to secure housing accommodation for the homeless, a step rendered necessary by reason of the unsuitability of the Shelters both from a sanitary and family point of view.

A Housing Sub-Committee, consisting of Councillors Croot (Chairman), Filmer, Gray and Holland, with Miss Kerrison and Mr. J.J. Harding, representing the Emergency Committee, was formed, and they were entrusted with the duty of removing and re-housing the homeless.

An Enquiry Office was opened at the Public Hall, and the Committee was fortunate in securing the valuable services of Miss E. Rutledge and Mr. J. Gibbons, Head Teachers of West Silvertown School, who did exceedingly good work, Miss Rutledge remaining until the office was closed on 26th July, 1917.

Fortunately for the Committee they were able to obtain, through the good offices of the Local Government Board, the use of 53 tenements belonging to the Port of London Authority on their Prince Regent Lane Estate, whilst a number of the bungalows erected by the Government at Plumstead and Eltham were also placed at the disposal of the Committee, but the reluctance of the workpeople to remove any distance from their work prevented practically any use being made of the latter dwellings and other available accommodation situated some distance from Silvertown.

Other premises, mostly the dwelling house portions of shops, which were closed, were taken in the Southern portion of the Borough, and by these means sufficient accommodation was found for those actually in need of assistance. A feature of the housing question was the fact that many of the poorer people took in and gave shelter to some of the refugees, and to this extent the Committee were relieved of their responsibilities.

At the beginning of March the houses in Silvertown began to be ready for re-occupation and from that time up to the end of July, 791 removals were carried out by the Council's own vehicles and men and by local contractors, 391 cases being removals to Silvertown, and by the middle of August the whole of the premises which had been taken temporarily were vacated, and all bedding, hired and lent, was after fumigation, sold to people in the area affected or returned to the firms hiring and the Institutions lending. This represented not less than 3,000 articles, and valuable assistance was rendered in numerous ways by the Stable Manager (Mr. G. Morse) and his Staff, and the Steward and Staff of the Plaistow Fever Hospital.

This branch of the work involved many visits to applicants and to premises offered, representing approximately 1,000 visits, which was made largely possible by the kindness of Messrs. Brunner Mond & Co. in lending one of their motor cars.

From the 6th March to the 26th July applications by various kinds numbered in all 1,735, and the number of letters written 847, and many warm expressions of appreciation of the work done by those in charge of the office were received.

The work of superintending the transference of the people from Silvertown to the houses provided for their accommodation, and their subsequent removal back again, was undertaken by Mr. J.J. Harding, and your Committee express their warmest thanks to him for the energy which he threw into the work and the success which attended his efforts. The work was arduous in the extreme, but was carried out with characteristic enthusiasm.

The Committee had various suggestions made to them for finding convalescent homes for the children who were injured and suffering from shock, and who were distributed in various Homes, found mainly through the instrumentality of the Emergency Committee, Miss Howard, of the Invalid and Crippled Children's Committee, and the Marie Celeste Samaritan Society of the London Hospital, and eventually the Hospital's Convalescent Home, 'Parkwood,' Swanley, was inspected, by Mr. Madden and Miss Ware, and found to be an Institution built and endowed by Mr. Peter Reid, for the accommodation of 120 adult convalescent patients from several London Hospitals. The building stands at the top of a hill in beautifully wooded grounds of 70 acres. It was found not only sufficiently spacious to accommodate 300 children but also large enough to provide class rooms for the partial continuance of their education. The Home had been temporarily closed owing to the difficulty in finding adequate nursing Staff. His Worship the Mayor (Mr. Alderman Mansfield) and the Chairman of the Education Committee (Mr. Alderman Enos Smith) had an interview with the Trustees of the Institution, with the result that these gentlemen, in a public spirited manner, handed the Home over to the Corporation for a period of three months, free of rent, rates and taxes, together with the services of the Matron, Assistant Matron, Nursing Sister and the Medical Officer. An agreement embodying these terms and other necessary details was entered into, after it had been ascertained that the Local Government Board had sufficient funds in hand, subscribed by the generous public, aided by a grant from H.M. Treasury. These negotiations took some little time, and subsequently it was necessary to get together the requisite Staff to run the establishment. The management being left in the capable hands of Miss Campbell, the Matron, that lady very soon had the requisite personnel. The Corporation lent two of their Engineers to work the boilers, and bedding from Dagenham, and additional beds and extra bedding were found, with the kindly assistance of Mr. Oxley, of the Local Government Board, and the furniture for the class rooms was provided by the Education Committee. The choosing of the children and the interviewing of the parents was undertaken by Miss Ware, who also was responsible for their transport to and from Swanley. At the commencement, the Metropolitan Asylums Board were good enough to permit the Committee to use their Motor Ambulances, but as time went on petrol became scarcer and the difficulties greater; not too great, however, for Miss Ware to overcome without the slightest mishap. Many of the children were examined by Dr. Sanders and Dr. Skerret before they went to Swanley. In spite of every precaution, however, Measles broke out shortly after the children's arrival. The first few cases were brought back to Plaistow or sent to the local hospital at Dartford, but as the complaint was very prevalent at the time, there was not sufficient accommodation at either of these places for the increased number of cases and in consequence, an isolation ward was opened in the Institution. Considering that at the time of the outbreak there were

over 240 children at Swanley, it speaks most highly for the very
excellent arrangements and the care taken by the Matron and her
assistants, when it is stated that the total number of cases was only
24. Although accommodation was provided for 300, this number,
for various reasons, but principally on account of the measles, was
never reached, the average number at the Institution throughout the
period, which by the graciousness of the Trustees was extended to
the 20th July (five months in all), being about 220.

The reports (brought up in the appendix) of Miss Campbell and
Miss Ware give an idea of the life children led.

The Mayor and the Chairman of the Education Committee
made frequent visits to the Home, and were most solicitous for the
welfare of the children.

The Committee, when they visited the Home in July last, could
not help being struck by the wonderful improvement in the
physique and well-being of the children in general, and think this
was due to the kindly and sympathetic treatment they received at
the hands of Miss Campbell, Miss Thomson and Sister Toyne, and
the splendid regime under which they lived. It was with pleasure
that the Committee were able to ask these ladies to accept a small
souvenir as a tangible recognition of the Committee's appreciation,
and they recommend that the heartiest of thanks of the Council be
accorded to them for all their invaluable services.

The thanks of the Committee are also due to Alderman Enos
Smith (Chairman of the Education Committee), who was most
assiduous in furthering the efforts made for the welfare of the children, and to Miss Ware, who spared neither time nor energy in her
efforts to ensure the comfort and being of the Silvertown children,
efforts which your Committee know were thoroughly appreciated
by the parents and the children themselves. The latter will no
doubt, always look back with pleasure to the good time they spent
at Swanley, and think of Miss Ware, Miss Williams and their
Teachers as real friends at a distressing time.

The Committee unanimously recommend the Council to adopt
the following resolution and they request the Trustees' acceptance

thereof, suitably engrossed and framed as a permanent record of their public-spirited action, for placing in their Committee Room at Swanley:-

The Mayor, Alderman and Burgesses of the County Borough of West Ham acting by the Council, hereby place on record their grateful appreciation of the public-spirited action of the Trustees of the Parkwood Convalescent Home, Swanley, Kent, in placing their Institution, free of rent, rates and taxes, and with the valuable services of the Matron, Miss Campbell, the Assistant Matron, Miss Thomson, Nursing Sister Miss Toyne and the Medical Officer of Health, Dr. Smith, at the disposal of the Committee appointed to deal with matters arising out of the Explosion at Silvertown on the 19th January, 1917.

During the period from 1st March, 1917, to 28th July, 1917, 387 convalescent and homeless children were maintained and educated to their incalculable benefit by means of funds given by a generous public aided by a Grant from H.M. Treasury.

They recommend that a suitable letter be sent to the various Institutions and individuals mentioned in this report, expressing the Council's admiration and gratitude for the invaluable and willing services so freely and ungrudgingly performed by them.

Whilst the negotiation were proceeding for the use of Swanley Home, arrangements were made to send 50 of the children to the Council's Convalescent Home, at the Grange, Harold Wood.

Miss Burrus, the Head Mistress of the Silvertown School, took charge of the children, and was very successful in her efforts to make them thoroughly comfortable and happy whilst at the Home. They remained there for a period of about 10 weeks, when a number of them were transferred to Swanley, until that Institution was closed. The expenditure incurred was just under £250.

Interim Accounts prepared by the Borough Treasurer are brought up in the Appendix. A final statement cannot be presented at this date, as one or two items still remain unpaid, but the additional expenditure will not be large.

Grateful thanks are also tendered to the Hon. Secretaries of the Emergency Committee, Miss Towers and Mr. J.J. Harding, upon whom fell the difficult task of organisation in its initial stages, for their valuable and indefatigable work.

The Committee fully realise the additional work willingly undertaken by the Town Clerk and his Staff, and record their appreciation of the services rendered by them, and they also thank all the various officials and employees who worked so admirably in their respective spheres.

In conclusion, the Committee unanimously adopted a vote of thanks to the Mayor for the able manner in which he presided over the many meetings which it was found necessary to hold, and for the time and interest he devoted to all measures for the assistance of the Explosion victims.

(Signed) R. MANSFIELD
Chairman
1st November, 1917.

Report of Miss Ware

Note: Miss Annie Ware was one of two West Ham Council Inspectors of Education.

The Explosion at Silvertown on January 19th 1917 rendered many families homeless and partially destroyed one school. Many children though not actually needing medical treatment, suffered severely from nervous shock. Immediately all philanthropic organisations dealt with these sad cases while many Teachers took charge of small children, housing, feeding and caring for them until definite arrangements could be made for their welfare.

Early in February a magnanimous offer by the Governors of the exquisite Convalescent Home, Parkwood, Swanley, Kent, with the spacious dormitories, bathrooms, dining and recreation rooms, and beautiful grounds, for the West Silvertown children for at least three months was gratefully accepted by the Mayor.

The Matron, Miss Campbell, and the Sisters of the Home held out a cheery welcome to the plan, anxious to extend a skilled hand and sympathetic touch of the sufferers in this great crisis. Throughout the Matron has been magnificent.

In February personal visits to those parents who could be traced resulted in their gladly availing themselves of the opportunity of placing their children in such comfortable surroundings, the confidence being strengthened by the knowledge that the Teachers had agreed to reside with the children.

At the end of February arrangements were complete. By the kind co-operation of the Metropolitan Asylums Board Motor Ambulances were placed at the disposal of the Committee, and on March 1st, 100 children were transferred from the Public Hall, Canning Town, to Parkwood, and on March 3rd, 150 children followed. Since that date small sections have at intervals joined the party, the total number admitted being 387 from Silvertown and (at a later date) ten small children from Poplar.

Dr Sanders, Medical Officer for West Ham, personally examined large sections of children, and was ably seconded by Dr. Skerrett. By this means as little infection as possible was assured, yet in spite of this there were several cases of measles.

Nine children were removed to Dartford or Plaistow Hospital, but when other children were attacked, the Matron opened an Isolation Ward, under the charge of Nurse Fraser (School Nurse). The cases were all of severe type, yet all made an excellent recovery.

SISTER THOMPSON taxed her brain to feed the children suitably. It was quite amusing to see the tiny tots go to the hatchway for a second helping, especially of any favourite dish.

SISTER TOYNE has been most sympathetic in the dressing of wounds and treatment of minor ailments, and all have endeavoured to make the children feel at home.

DR. SMITH, MEDICAL OFFICER OF PARKWOOD, visited the home daily when necessary.

The Educational work, as well as that of the Orderly Staff, was organised by Miss Emmeline Williams, Head Mistress of West Silvertown Infants' School and the undermentioned ladies faithfully and harmoniously and untiringly carried out her instructions:

Miss McDougall, Miss O'Neill, Miss Critten, Miss Poore, Miss Clarke, Miss Lethaby, Miss Foote, Miss Turner, Miss Brown, Mrs Polson.

The DUTIES OF THE ORDERLY STAFF demanded greater self-sacrifice as the undermentioned shows:-

Breakfast, 6 a.m.

In Wards 7 a.m. to 7.45 a.m. Children's dressing time.

7.50 a.m. The youngest children enter Dining Hall to be well placed before the bigger children arrived.

8 a.m. Children's Breakfast.

8.30 a.m. Morning Prayer and Hymn in Chapel.

8.40 a.m. to 9. Free play.

12.30 p.m. Children's Dinner.

1 p.m. to 2.15 p.m. Supervision of free play. Preparation of children for walk.

4.45 to 5 p.m. Prepare Children for Tea.

5 p.m. Children's Tea.

5.30 p.m. Evening Prayer and Hymn in Chapel.

6 p.m. Small children bathed and put to bed.

6.30 to 7 p.m. Remaining children bathed and put to bed.

The TEACHING STAFF observed the ordinary School Hours, and when possible lessons were taken in the open air.

The children welcomed the discipline and the lessons. Careful and sensible work is shown in the Exercise Books. Composition breathes of an intelligent appreciation of the sylvan surroundings and happy home life of Parkwood.

Intense interest was shown in the development of the buds and various spring flowers, hence drawing, colouring and collecting specimens for preservation became a keen delight to them all.

One of the voluntary helpers has many pets and on various occasions invited the children to see young rabbits, chickens and calves, much to their enlightened enjoyment.

Needlework, including mending of garments, has been a constant care and tax upon the energies of the Staff.

Eighty-eight over-all suits have been made. The first twenty were worked by the girls themselves for drill costumes. These proved so popular that an arrangement was made for any who liked to have them at the cost of the material. Sixty-four suits have been paid for.

The Bathing at night was at first a problem. When the elder girls had been trained to render efficient help it became possible for every child to be bathed every day.
The children love their baths now. Even the youngest and most timid are sad if for any reason night bath has to be missed.

There is a fine *esprit de corps*; all take a keen interest in races and field games.

The older boys and girls are very good to the little ones. Ten little Poplar children were gladly welcomed by all and settled down quite happily, especially as the elder girls asked to 'mother them' in the dormitories.

During the hot weather the children have liked to spend much of their playtime in the woods. One of the chief games has been the planting of houses formed from fallen branches, twigs, stones, and other things found in the woods; it has been interesting to note that a 'bathroom' has been a common feature of all these plans.

The beautiful rhododendrons and azaleas were a perfect revelation while the lovely avenue of pines leading from the entrance gates to almost the lawn afforded much comment. They were all seen 'snow clad' in March, fresh and green in Spring and Summer.

Some children said they would like to see them 'dressed for Christmas.'

Easter Monday was a real holiday. How the children enjoyed seeking for the Easter eggs hidden in the grounds! Each child secured one, and then enjoyed games on the lawn. After Tea, games, dances and a little play by the elder girls, songs by the Matron and her friends were much enjoyed by children and visitors.

On Whitsun Monday sports again were held, the boys being entertained by visitors who played cricket with them.

In July a 'raspberry' tea was given to the children on the lawn, and on July 18th all the voluntary helpers were entertained similarly by the little people, when a very happy time was spent.

On July 19th, His Worship the Mayor of West Ham, Alderman Mansfield accompanied by members of the Council and the Emergency Committee visited the Home, and all were pleased to see the great improvement in the appearance of the children. Their hair (thanks to the untiring efforts of Nurse Fraser) looked healthy and bright, their flesh also white and firm, while the natural manners and winning ways excited pleasing comment. The songs, games and dances were again given on the lawn, and were very much appreciated.

Before the Mayor and the other visitors departed a very happy gathering, in which His Worship spoke in high appreciation of the valuable work of the Matron and Hospital Staff and the Teaching Staff, took place on one of the Recreation Rooms.

When the party left hearty cheers came from the windows of the dormitories where the children in their night attire were watching the departure of the Motors.

The children return to West Silvertown School in sections beginning on July 23rd and ending on July 26th, the journey being taken by road.

21st July 1917.

(Signed) ANNIE M. WARE.

Report of Miss Campbell
Matron of the Hospital Convalescent Home,
Parkwood, Swanley

The Home opened on March 1st, 1917, for the reception of children from the West Silvertown School. On that date 100 children were admitted. On March 3rd, 142 children followed.

During the ensuing fortnight parents of some of the children came and removed them. Their reasons for doing this varied, but the most general was that the children had written saying they were homesick, felt the cold, did not like the food, and wished to go home.

The first case of measles appeared on March 5th. The total number of cases was 22. Of these, nine were nursed in the Home. The others were removed to the Isolation Hospital, Dartford, and the West Ham Fever Hospital. One case of diphtheria occurred in a girl two days after admission. She was removed to the isolation Hospital, Dartford.

Six fresh batches of children have been received since March 3rd. On July 12th 10 children were admitted from the Upper North Street, Poplar. 397 children have passed through the Home during the five months. The largest number at one time being 242 on March 3rd, and 236 at present date.

The nursing staff in the employment of the West Ham Borough Council has consisted of one Night Sister, for the first three months, one Assistant Nurse, one V.A.D. Nurse, one helper, resident, one helper, non-resident. The West Ham Borough Council Nurse sent by Dr. Sanders has had the care of the children's heads and the supervision of their personal cleanliness. She has been assisted by the Teachers on orderly duty, by the Sister employed by the Trustees of the Home for the sick children, and by the two Nurses. In addition, the Matron appealed to ladies in the neighbourhood for help with the evening bathing. The following ladies volunteered to come on certain evenings each week, and have been of great help:-

Miss Cockburn, Mrs. Osmond, Mrs. Matthews, Miss C. Simmonds, Miss Macraw, Miss Steele, Miss Trill, Mrs. Waring, Miss Starr, Miss E. Mathews

The task of cleansing the children after their admission and of keeping them clean in person and clothing has been an arduous one, and without the diligence and perseverance of all concerned it could not have been carried out with the thoroughness it required.

The question of clothing the children necessitated appealing for clothes, as well as asking the Corporation for money for materials. The first gift came through them, and consisted of shirts, stockings and shoes, which were gratefully received. Thanks are due to the following for presents of clothing:-

Mrs. du Croz, Rooksbury, Weybridge; Mrs. and Miss Payne, Hilmarton Vicarage, Calne, Wilts.; Miss Wilton, Heathlands, Chadwell Heath; Mr. Silcock. 21, Brecknock Road, N.; Mrs. C. Atkins, Lancaster Cottage, Weybridge; Mrs. Crawford, Orchard Lee, Swanley Junction; Miss Jordan, The London Hospital.

A Working Party was organised at Parkwood by Mrs. de Spailier, Miss Simmonds, Miss C. Simmonds, Mrs. Finn, Mrs. Field, Mrs. Stares. Many useful garments were made. As summer drew near, cotton material was bought for light costumes. Many of the parents have been willing to pay for these. Boot repairs have been done, and the parents have been asked to pay for these as well. Altogether £26 9s. 3d. has been paid by the Matron for clothing and boot repairs. Parents have refunded £16 0s. 3d.

The children's amusements have not been forgotten. Mr. J.W. Hope, of Messrs. Knights' Soap Works, sent on behalf of the Silvertown Manufacturers, cheques to the amount of £16 4s. 5d. for toys and amusements. We thank them for this generous gift. Thanks are due also to the following for contributions of toys, games, books and puzzles:-

The Mayor of West Ham; Mrs. Leopold Wood, Hazeldine, Swanley Junction; Mrs. Simmonds, Birchwood, Swanley Junction; Mrs. Allnutt, Crockenhill Road, Swanley Junction; Mrs. Stares, The Limes, Swanley Junction; Mrs. J. Wood, The Mount, Swanley Junction; Mrs. T. Wood, Zounds Lodge, Crockenhall; Mrs. Reed, Allington, Swanley Junction; Master J. Simmonds, Valetta, Temple, Ewell; Mrs. Simmonds, Highclure, Kenley; Mrs. Oswald Vinson, Ruxley Manor, Foots Cray; Miss Callingham, Park House, Thames Ditton; Mrs. Davis, Highlands Farm, Swanley.

Some of the toys are being taken back by Miss Williams, to be given to the children after their return, as there were too many for them to get through while they were here. Miss Simmonds and Miss Callingham's gift took the form of 10s. each, to be spent on prizes and gifts for good work in helping in the Home.

Up to the present date 14 notices of air raids have been given by the Police to the Matron. The Staff have been on duty for six occasions for the greater part of the night. The children have had no cause for alarm, and have not even been aware that anything unusual was going on. The Special Constables and the Swanley Volunteer Force have assisted the staff at night by sending six members each to patrol the building, and be in readiness in case of alarm. Mr. Cecil Cockburn has undertaken the arrangements with the two sets of Volunteers. He and his brother, Mr. James Cockburn, are particularly deserving of thanks for their promptness in getting quickly to the Home on each occasion, and the real interest they have taken in the children's safety.

The Medical Officer has attended the Home twice weekly for minor ailments among the children, but there has been very little for him to do, as they have been remarkably well. Thirteen children were sent to West Ham to have their eyes examined by Dr. Sanders. Twelve were supplied with glasses.

The Chaplain of the Home has held two services in the Chapel for the children each Sunday, and has had a special service and catechising every Wednesday. There has been additional services for the Staff. For the first two Sundays in March the services were taken by the Rev. A. W. F. de Spailier, Chaplain of St. Bartholomew's Hospital Convalescent Home, Swanley Junction, and a week-day service was taken by the Rev. J. Jellicoe, Vicar of Swanley, the Chaplain being detained by duties elsewhere.

The Head Teacher, Miss Williams, has conducted the management of the children and the staff of Teachers to the entire satisfaction of the Matron. She has spared no pains to make the undertaking a success. Her right sense of duty, her devotion to the children, and her tact in dealing with the various difficulties that have come in her way, have claimed the confidence and respect of all who have worked with her.

The Teachers have undertaken the unusual work put upon them with goodwill. They have never failed in their care for the children, and have done all in their power to make them happy. Nurse Fraser has been a great help, and has always shown herself cheerful and willing in carrying out her duties.

Parkwood, Swanley, Kent.
July 17th, 1917.

Mayor of West Ham Silvertown Explosion Fund
Cash Statement (Interim)

25th October 1917

	£	s.	d.		£	s.	d.		£	s.	d.
RECEIPTS											
Cash per His Worship the Mayor											
(National Relief Fund)									5000	0	0
Total									5000	0	0
EXPENDITURE											
Temporary Assistance, Cash									1563	0	2
Food, Clothing, Fuel, Lighting,											
Equipment, Labour &c:-											
Hermit Road School					171	2	2				
Cory Institute					97	9	9				
Lees Hall					93	0	3				
St. Matthew's Hostel					79	5	10				
Barking Road Tabernacle					65	0	3				
Invalid Kitchens of London					65	0	0				
Swanscombe Street School					51	2	1				
Seamen's Rest					41	11	9				
Poplar and Stepney Sick Asylums					40	16	0				
St. Gabriel's Vicarage					38	8	11				
West Ham Workhouse					17	19	8				
Mansfield House Settlement					16	13	2				
Poplar Workhouse					15	9	8				
St. Margaret's Roman Catholic Schools					15	9	0				
West Ham Vicarage					13	4	11				
St. Barnabas' Parsonage					11	6	9				
Mary Street Church					1	10	6				
Blankets for Refugees Centres	53	3	0								
Less Sold	15	14	0								
					37	8	2				
Total									871	18	10
Chemist, Red Cross, &c.									8	3	5
Funeral Expenses									523	6	6
Furniture									876	7	6
Furniture Removals (excluding services											
of Council's Stables Department)									422	14	2
Rents, Rates of Houses for											
Temporary Accommodation	861	9	0								
Less Rents Received	303	9	6								
									557	19	6
Fuel, Light, Repairs and Cleaning											
– Houses, &c.									9	17	1
Clothing for Patients leaving Hospital									4	7	7

Administrative Expenses:-

Stationery		18	11	1				
Travelling		10	8	2				
Petrol		1	0	6				
					29	19	9	
Total		4867	14	6				
Cash at Bank and in hand					132	5	6	
					5000	0	0	

C.H. PATTERSON, Borough Treasurer, 25th October, 1917.

Silvertown Explosion Fund
Parkwood Convalescent Home (Swanley) Account Interim

19th January to 20th October, 1917

	£	s.	d.
RECEIPTS			
Government Grants	2000	0	0
Parents' Contributions	219	0	0
Sale of Clothing	21	10	3
	2240	10	3
Balance, being deficiency at this date	33	9	5
	2273	19	8

	£	s.	d.
PAYMENTS			
Honoraria to the Staff and Teachers engaged at Swanley	118	19	6
Wages of Servants	554	4	2
Provisions	1205	2	11
Fuel, Light and Cleaning	82	5	10
Furniture and Repairs to Furniture	53	18	6
Cartage of Furniture	24	6	6
Conveyance of Children and other Travelling Expenses	101	3	0
Clothing	65	18	11
Insurance	2	14	3
Maintenance of Children in Fever Hospital	30	7	3
Printing, Stationery, Postages, &c.	29	13	10
Legal Expenses (Trustees' Solicitors)	5	5	0
	2273	19	8

Unpaid accounts in hand, £40

C.H. Patterson, Borough Treasurer
Borough Treasurer's Department, West Ham, 20th October, 1917.

CHAPTER 4
ESSEX VOLUNTEER REGIMENT

Note: *The following is taken from the regimental magazine produced after the explosion.*

1st Battalion Essex Volunteer Regiment Magazine
No. 16, February 1917

Our Effort in the Great Explosion

The West Ham Companies of the 1st Essex Volunteer Battalion fully justified their existence and the time, money and care expended on their training, by the part they have taken in the great explosion.

Within a few minutes of the nature of the calamity becoming known, our fellows began to roll up, and in a short time Capt. Mann was at the head of a willing squad, anxious to perform any duty allotted to them, the picquets and most of the party sticking to it till the morning was well advanced.

On the Saturday Plat. Commanders Paul, Starling, and Hawes, with a party from B Company, were active from midday till past midnight, being joined later by Commanders Parrack and Wilkinson, and a party from H Coy.

On Sunday quite half the Companies fell out from trench parade, volunteering to render assistance, but only a dozen were allowed to go, under Plat. Com Starling. These were augmented almost every hour, until large parties of both B and H Companies were actively engaged. Some were making up beds, others attending refugees, others looking after the food, others were busy finding missing members of families, in some cases digging among the ruins for hours before meeting with success.

And the Ambulance! What a work they did! Sergt.-Major May and the Ambulance of the 1st, augmented by sections from the 5th and the Red Cross nurses, as well as the Women's Reserve Ambulance with their motors, were at it night and day. As one well known gentleman remarked – perhaps we had better not say whom – 'It makes one proud to be a Britisher, when such whole-souled work is voluntarily given to help the distressed.'

Nor can we overlook the Motor and Cyclist Sections. It was truly wonderful how the organisation worked. Cars seemed to come from everywhere, and to be in every spot where help was required. To these two Sections – not yet officially recognised, we believe – many a victim owes his or her life to-day.

Early in the week a Battalion order was issued, the Mayor having expressed a desire for further assistance, and all-night picquets have been provided by each of the Companies night by night. But, in addition to this, squads of men under officers or non-coms. have been coming forward every day, rendering help wherever needed. Truly the 1st Essex Volunteer Regiment has justified itself.

In connection with the Public Funeral on the 30th, of Sub-Officer Vickers and Fireman Sell, who lost their lives in this catastrophe, a detachment comprising members of all the Companies of the 1st Battalion attended under command of Captain Fisher (B Coy.). The other officers attending were Capt Moore (D Coy.), Capt. Mann (H Coy.), Plat. Coms. Hamilton, Hawes and Paul and Plat. Coms. Bowl and Tomlinson. The Battalion are proud to have had the privilege of testifying by their presence their appreciation of the services rendered at all times by the members of the Fire Brigade Service, with whom they have for so many months worked in conjunction.

CHAPTER 5

EAST END SETTLEMENTS

Mansfield House University Settlement and Canning Town Women's Settlement were part of a wider movement to bring education, welfare and culture to the poor areas of London, particularly the East End.

Mansfield House University Settlement was founded in 1889 by students connected with Mansfield College, Oxford. At first the settlement was housed in two small shops in Barking Road, but by 1900 Fairburn Hall also in Barking Road had been built.

Canning Town Women's Settlement was founded in 1892 by F.W. Newland. Their headquarters were at Lees Hall in Barking Road and by 1910 there was a settlement house in Cumberland Road, Plaistow, as well. Miss Rebecca Cheetham was the first warden of the Settlement, from 1892 to 1917.

MANSFIELD HOUSE UNIVERSITY SETTLEMENT

The Explosion
Mansfield House Magazine, February 1917

Once again Settlements have been called upon to render special service in an emergency. Our readers will have seen in the newspapers accounts of the terrific explosion which occurred in the East End of London on the evening of Jan. 19th. Windows were broken for a great distance round, and Settlement premises amongst many others were damaged in this way; but fortunately there were no injuries to persons except, at one of our buildings, a few cuts from broken glass. A children's party was in progress at another building, but the ladies in charge showed great coolness and presence of mind, and there was no great panic. Very soon everyone was at work helping to receive the refugees from the shattered area. Some fifty homeless persons were accommodated that night in the Residence; those who were injured were put to bed; whilst the others sat round the fire in the Reception Room. It was a terribly anxious night for many of them, families were scattered; and conversation was largely of missing husbands or injured children. Accommodation was found for a far larger number of refugees on the premises of the neighbouring Women's Settlement.

The following day the Mayor of the Borough in which the explosion occurred called together a meeting at which an Emergency Committee was formed to deal with the immediate situation. The Warden and Mr. Mess are both serving on the Committee, which has also representatives from the two other Settlements. One of the first things to be done was to find temporary accommodation for all the homeless persons – no easy task in an already overcrowded East End district. It was decided to house people for a time in various church and chapel rooms, kindly placed at the disposal of the Committee, and in a public elementary school. Some six hundred in all were so accommodated.

Already, owing to the Marie Celeste Samaritan Society of the London Hospital and other friends, more than two hundred children have been sent to convalescent homes in the country. There is some possibility that the children and teachers from the public elementary school most seriously damaged by the explosion will be transferred for some months to a large convalescent home in Kent.

All day Saturday offers of help were received and voluntary workers kept coming in. An information bureau was opened and a register of persons and families affected by the explosion was compiled. Lists of killed and injured were obtained from hospitals and mortuaries. In a very large number of cases the Bureau was the means of helping persons to obtain news of their families or of friends. There were some touching reunions. Sometimes, alas! the bureau brought bad news to those who consulted it. But we are glad to say that the casualty list has proved to be much smaller than was at first anticipated. The official list is as follows:-

	Men	Women	Children	Total
Killed	44	11	14	69
Seriously injured	19	34	19	72
Slightly injured	155	102	71	328

In addition to the Emergency Committee there has been formed, at the request of the Local Government Board, a sub-committee of the Borough Council to administer relief and to attempt to find permanent quarters for those still homeless. We are glad to report that in response to urgent representations the Local Government Board has approved a fairly generous scale of temporary relief. The Ministry of Munitions has opened an office at the Public Library, Broadway, Plaistow, to deal with claims for compensation.

The distress caused by the explosion is very great, and the difficulties presented are many; but this emergency like many others has shown what great resources of goodwill there are in the community to draw upon at need.

We understand that for certain 'out of pocket' expenses connected with this relief work the Settlement will be repaid from public funds. In these emergencies, however there are always some expenses which cannot be formally rendered in any statement of accounts, to say nothing of the heavy wear and tear of the Settlement buildings. If some of our well-to-do friends, unable to render personal service, can send us special donations, we shall be very glad to receive them.

The Explosion
Mansfield House Magazine, March 1917

Even a disaster like the explosion on January 19th has its compensations. The elementary school nearest the factory at which the explosion occurred is very badly damaged and cannot be used again for several months. Happily, arrangements have been made for some three hundred of the children from this school with their teachers, to be transferred to Park Wood, a beautiful convalescent home near Swanley, Kent. It is hoped that they will all be there by March 3rd. We are very glad that this proposal, to which we referred to last month, is being carried into effect. For once at least, some of our East End children will taste the joys of a boarding school in the country, and watch the coming of spring.

Hundreds of other children have been sent away to convalescent homes for short periods; the Invalid and Crippled Society, whose office is at Lees Hall has undertaken this side of the work. The burden on the ladies chiefly responsible has been very heavy.

The Emergency Committee has continued to render splendid service throughout February. The work of finding housing accommodation for homeless families has gone steadily forward. The Hall of our Boys' Club, in which some fifty women and girls were being accommodated, was vacated at the end of the first week. All other temporary 'shelters' were emptied a week or two later, with the exception of a Council School, which had to be used for some time longer, and has only just been given up. All the families who were rendered homeless have now found accommodation, but we understand that the houses which were obtained on the Port of London Authority's estate are only available for three months. There is also very serious overcrowding in the district generally. We have just heard, for instance, of a family of nine who were all sleeping in one room. In the wrecked area itself the work of repairing houses which were not too seriously damaged has been going forward rapidly, and a large percentage of the people who had to leave the district will shortly be able to return to their old homes, if they have not already done so. It has not been practicable, of course, in present circumstances to consider any scheme for remodelling the whole area on healthier lines.

Stories are already current to the effect that the Ministry of Munitions is not dealing generously with claims for compensation. A small committee has been appointed locally to look into the matter; we trust it will be found that the stories have but slender foundation.

We hope, too that landlords will deal fairly with their tenants. The position at law would appear to be that as long as the tenancy continues the tenant is liable for the full rent even though a part or the whole of the house is not habitable. It is tolerably certain that no Court could be found, in present circumstances, to enforce such a claim.

We hope that the remarks made by the Coroner at the adjourned inquest will finally dispose of the wild rumours which have been current in many quarters as to casualties. There is now no ground whatever for doubting the substantial accuracy of the official figures. They are indeed sufficiently tragic: some seventy-five people were killed and several hundreds injured; but everyone who saw the actual wreckage in the devastated area will agree that they are much smaller than might have been supposed.

CANNING TOWN WOMEN'S SETTLEMENT

Minutes 21st February 1917
Miss Cheetham's Report

That owing to the terrible Explosion which took place on January 19th in the East End, practically all the normal work of the Settlement was suspended for the first fortnight, and we were thankful to be in a position to be able to give immediate help to many before the official relief work was set up. Over 300 women and children were sheltered in Lees Hall the first night, first aid was rendered to the injured, and a Register of names opened. Besides our own workers, many of our women and girls gave splendid help. Miss Searle had the whole of the catering in her hands, and provided some hundreds of meals. Miss Towers was Hon. Sec. of the Emergency Committee and Miss Cheetham was appointed Treasurer of the Emergency Relief Fund which realized about £350. Through the generous kindness of the London Hospital, the Salvation Army, the Church Army, and many private individuals, over 300 children have been sent away. The Borough Schools suffered disastrously, two were completely wrecked and 19 were closed the first week. Most of the families are being housed temporarily until their own homes are rebuilt.

That Danbury had not been let, as they had been glad to use it for victims of the explosion.

CHAPTER 6
SAILORTOWN

This is an extract from Sailortown, *a pamphlet by Revd G.H. Mitchell, who was a Chaplain in the Port of London and Chaplain to the Mariners Friends Society.*

The Great Explosion

The biggest disaster since the Great Fire of London in 1666 took place in a munition factory recently in Sailortown.

Many were appalled at the magnitude of the explosion and the newspaper reports were by no means imaginary. I personally went over the scene of the disaster the next day and witnessed the aftermath of destruction. Dante's 'Inferno' could not have made this aftermath more vivid. 'Indescribable!' is the word used by the manager of one factory destroyed. And, indeed no pen can possibly describe the desolation and destruction that I witnessed with my own eyes as I walked through the fated district.

A large crowd of anxious sightseers were kept waiting hopelessly for admission into the doomed area. My official passport into dockland obtained for me permission to pass through – I beheld and wondered! What evil sprite had been here at work? Surely this is not the work of man and it is assuredly not the work of God.

Facing me was one measureless wilderness of primeval savagery. Smoking fields, once fertile with busy life, now ploughed up by fierce and angry fiends. Where once stood a fire station there was now a heap of bricks; a batch of new houses was demolished absolutely. Where once stood majestic buildings of commercial activity and engineering science, there remained nothing but fields inundated with ghastly holes like the craters of an earthquake.

Small houses in some streets were simply not – or at least, there remained nothing but fragmentary indications that they were once the abode of little children and strong men, mothers and work-girls. I went into several of these sad remains, and chatted with tearful men and women. Some had miraculous escapes – one family had just gone into the yard to watch the fire when their home was demolished, and they were not hurt.

Alas! many had not escaped, but lay 'unhonoured and unsung' amid the ruins of this strange escapade of mysterious and cruel fate.

The fire was still smouldering in some parts, burning slowly as if exhausted by the fury of the night. I stood within twenty yards of a burning tank, and felt not afraid – Death, indeed had no terrors then. As I heard one woman say: 'No we're not going away; we have met the trouble so far, we'll stick it now.'

Again I descended into big holes and clambered over the conglomeration of iron boilers, bricks and scarlet mud, and I imagined a primeval forest rent asunder by some furious gale. I saw in the midst a cap – nothing more that indicated any sign of the life that once had been.

Strange irony of the gods! Within twenty yards of the actual place of disaster were some forty chickens, gaily strutting to and fro, finding what food they could; while about the same distance in another direction was a great boiler, lying in the middle of the road, bent and twisted like an uncanny octopus exhausted in its struggle for existence.

And I saw one woman hugging to her bosom a live grey kitten that had been saved the greater fate. And, again, I was moved to pity as I watched a picture of the infant Christ in one bedroom, all askew, looking on at all this ghastliness and death.

Specials and ambulance men more than justified their existence – serried ranks of specials moved solemnly from post to post, and the ambulance men carried away the silent dead. At the end, so far as one could draw a boundary line, was the remains of an iron church, while opposite that a once flourishing public-house in ruins – and, in the corner, a fallen clock, the hands of which pointed on the seven. A number of the 'boys', cold and weary, were importunate in the demands for hot tea and coffee, but the smiling proprietor declared she had no cups left, though there was plenty of tea.

Still another house offered me a view through a hole where a window once was, and I saw a little chap, about thirteen, sitting in front of a slow burning fire with his knees drawn up and his hand buried in his hands, as if in meditation or asleep.

On this night one young man was leaving a local factory in company with his sister. But they were parted, and the sister arrived home in safety, while the brother was missing. Hospital were searched in vain, and given up for lost. On the fourth night to the joy of the family, he returned home safe and well – a fallen beam had pinned him down and his cries for help were unheard for a time. Unconscious, he was finally taken to an obscure cottage, and was afterwards little the worse for his experience.

The long, long trail had ended sadly for some of the boys; not only those fighting in the trenches and on the mighty deep, but for many in the homeland too – the great explosion terminated the trail of some on that terrible night.

I visited the 'hero policeman' at the Poplar Hospital, and buried him amid honours jewelled with mourners tears. As an ex-P.C. this was a sad pleasure to me.

Sailortown has had its sorrows and hides a wealth of grief like the waves of the sea moaning lullabies of poignant pain. And yet she goes on 'living and loving,' working and waiting – waiting her emancipation from the ills that she is heir to.

The great explosion sent a thrill through her, the thrill of a mighty resolve to 'carry on' to the end.

CHAPTER 7
POLICE, AMBULANCE
AND HOSPITAL

METROPOLITAN POLICE

Police Heroism
The Police Review and Parade Gossip, 9th February 1917

The story of the devotion to duty, the heroism, and the self-sacrifice of Police-Constable George Greenoff, adds yet another chapter to the annals of a Force which has already added many names to
the roll of those who are 'faithful unto death.' The tale is a simple
one, and needs no adornment. P.C. Greenoff was on duty outside a
munitions factory near London, when a fire broke out in the building. He remained at his post to warn people of their danger, as an
explosion was imminent. Regardless of his own personal danger, he
devoted himself with all his energies to the task of getting as many
people as possible out of the burning building, and in preventing a
stampede. In this he was heroically occupied when the terrible
explosion occurred, with the result he was struck on the head by a
large missile, and from the effect of this and other injuries he died
in hospital a few days afterwards.

His Majesty the King has conveyed an expression of his sincere
sympathy to the hero's widow and family, together with an assurance of his 'sense of admiration that the best traditions of the Police
Force have been so nobly maintained in this signal act of courage
and devotion to duty.' For this gracious message, expressed with the

felicity of phrase which is so characteristic of His Majesty, not only to those whom it is directly addressed, but every Constable in the Service will feel grateful, and the more so because we may recognise that the King is speaking for his people as well as himself. As a nation we are indeed proud of our Police. We know that we have in them an army of protectors whose unflinching courage and high sense of duty rise superior to all emergencies, and enable them with steadfastness and heroism to face the perils of death itself. Of a surety Police Constable George Greenoff has not died in vain. To his heroic conduct many owe their lives to-day; from his heroic example those who are left to 'carry on' will draw fresh inspiration for the future.

ST JOHN AMBULANCE BRIGADE

SJAB magazine, *First Aid*, February 1917

THE GREAT EXPLOSION.—On Friday, January 19th, in the early hours of the evening, all London was startled by a loud roar, the sounds of which reached far beyond the confines of the metropolis. The cause was an explosion in a munition factory in the East End of London.

Although the air raid parties formed by the St. John Ambulance Brigade to deal with casualties in the event of a Zeppelin air raid on London (through no fault of the Brigade organisation) received no special summons, except in one or two cases several hours later, much good work was done, both by nursing sisters and men of the Brigade, who hurried to the spot from neighbouring districts. It will be very difficult to form an estimate of even the number of cases treated by the voluntary workers.

At one ambulance station, which had been organised some months before in the event of Zeppelin raids, some 150 cases were treated on the Friday evening by the surgeon, the Lady Superintendent and members of the Beckton Ambulance and

Nursing Divisions, assisted by some men belonging to other divisions. Individual men were working to rescue patients other portions of the large area affected by the explosion, and in spite of the difficulties of working at night, much good work was done in rescuing men, women and children, who unfortunately, in some cases were in a dying condition.

Transport provided by various agencies was utilised without pause being made to ascertain by whom it was furnished. The consequence was that the hospitals at that end of London were quickly crowded with patients, and some of the Brigade men were very busily engaged in assisting to dress injuries, working far into the night, and attending at the hospital for some hours on the two following days.

Other ambulance workers flocked to the scene of the explosion on the Saturday and Sunday and succeeding days, and assisted in removing bodies from the ruins, in the hope (nearly always in vain) that some persons might be found alive.

For a fortnight after the explosion the tent belonging to the Beckton Division was maintained at the scene of the disaster, many accidents which occurred to the military and others overhauling the ruins being treated.

The following is a report from the Stratford Express *of 23 April 1919 remembering the part played by the St John Ambulance Brigade in the aftermath of the explosion.*

Echo of Silvertown Explosion
Fine work by St. John Nurses and men

The Commissioner of No.1 District, St. John Ambulance Brigade, has presented two surgical haversacks to Beckton Nursing Division, and a stretcher and surgical haversack to Beckton Men's Division in recognition of services rendered on the occasion of the great explosion at Silvertown in Jan., 1917. Two officers and 23 nursing sisters and men were on duty that Friday night, some being there within fifteen minutes of the explosion, with a plentiful supply of bandages, dressings, etc. Duty was again rendered on the Saturday and Sunday, and on the Monday an ambulance tent was put up by the Beckton Division. With the assistance of East Ham and Forest Gate Divisions this was kept open night and day for a fortnight, during which period no fewer than 214 accidents were attended. A number of cases were of a serious nature and had to be removed to hospital. This total does not include the cases treated at the actual time of the explosion.

King George and Queen Mary visited the scene during this period and personally inspected the ambulance station and expressed their appreciation of the good work done.

The members of the Beckton Nursing and Men's Divisions have also kept open at St. John's Schools, North Woolwich, a dressing and temporary rest station since March 1916. This station was equipped and maintained through the generosity of the Silvertown and North Woolwich Patriotic Committee, under the personal supervision of Dr. Brews, Dr. Sampey and Dr. Hill, and since its opening nurses and men have attended in case of need through air raids every night. In all, the nurses and men have made 2,832 attendances during this time. The station was of great service at the time of the explosion, and was kept busy the whole of the night.

QUEEN MARY'S HOSPITAL FOR THE EAST END

Annual Report 1917

Over 100 victims of the terrible East End explosion, which occurred at the beginning of the year; were treated at the Hospital. Of these 25 were so badly injured that they had to be detained in the Hospital. Their Majesties the King and Queen sent a special messenger to enquire as to the nature of the injuries, who also conveyed a message of sympathy with the victims.

CHAPTER 8
ST BARNABAS' CHURCH, SILVERTOWN

This pamphlet was produced by the church shortly after the explosion as an aid to fundraising.

A short descriptive sketch, including an account of the Great Explosion of January 19, 1917, showing how the church life of the district was and is affected.

PART I

This little brochure will probably be read by many friends who are living amid pleasant rural or suburban surroundings and who have never heard of Silvertown, for even when the great disaster of January 19th, 1917, occurred, the locality was carefully camouflaged by 'DORA' [the Defence of the Realm Act, which enforced measures such as strict press censorship during the First World War].

Let me first paint a word picture of the district, particularly West Silvertown. It is buried away in the extreme East End of London, an overflow from London proper and forms part of the thickly populated district known as London-over-the-Border. It answers to the schoolboy's definition of an island, 'a piece of land surrounded entirely surrounded by water', for it is bounded on the south by the River Thames, on the north by the Victoria and Albert Docks and at either end by the entrances into the Docks from the river, the only connection with the 'mainland' being the swing bridges over these entrances. At certain times during the day and night, as the tide serves, these bridges are swung open to allow vessels of all types, from the little 'monkey' barge to the big cargo steamers, to enter or leave the Docks. I can imagine nothing more depressing than to be held up at the 'Bridge' after a hard day's work in factory or office, without shelter of any kind, on a rough November night, with a gale blowing from the south-west, bringing with it stinging showers of cold rain, and faced with the prospect of a wait of half an hour while a string of barges is being slowly piloted through the locks. This is what thousands of workpeople in the neighbourhood have to contend with.

The effect of this belt of water is completely to isolate West Silvertown socially. To run a tram or omnibus service along one main road is impracticable owing to the delays that would be occasioned not only by the swing bridges but also by the several level crossings.

Now let us take a walk through the district. The whole length of the river frontage is taken up by large factories, the output of which finds its way to all parts of the world. The names of the firms owning these factories are household words. These are the soap works of John Knight Limited, whose products, particularly the Royal Primrose Soap, are so well known; also the sugar refinery of Abram Lyle & Sons, Ltd. of 'golden syrup' fame; again, your car, if you are fortunate enough to possess one, is probably driven by the petrol from the large storage tanks close by. These are only a few of the links by which West Silvertown is connected with readers of this book.

Running parallel with the river, with the factories between, is the main road along which a constant stream of traffic is passing all day and far into the night, bringing the raw material to feed the factories and taking away the finished products. Between the main road and the Docks there is a narrow belt of land laid out in the streets of small dwellings which form the Ecclesiastical District of St. Barnabas. These provide housing accommodation for a population of four to five thousand, all of whom with few exceptions work in the locality.

The foregoing details may possibly have proved tedious to many readers, but it is necessary that they should have in their mind's eye a rough idea of the district to enable them to grasp the magnitude of the terrible catastrophe that overwhelmed it on that awful January evening, an account of which will be given in Part II.

PART II

A few minutes before seven on the evening of January 19th 1917, people who happened to be out of doors in London noticed a vivid red glow in the sky in an easterly direction. Many conjectures were made as to the origin, and the probability of a big fire having broken out being discussed when suddenly a column of flame shot up into the air, and almost simultaneously a low roar rent the air accompanied by the tinkling sound of broken glass as the concussion found its vent in all directions. The crowds in the street increased as the people rushed out of doors to ascertain what had happened, and many wild guesses· made: 'A Zeppelin raid!' 'A Zeppelin brought down!' It gradually became known that a tremendous explosion had occurred, but where? That was the difficulty, for the telephone and telegraph wires were destroyed and the district was entirely cut off from communication with the outside world, and the only means of locating the scene of the disaster was to make for the direction of the glare in the sky.

And what of Silvertown itself? Many of the people were standing at the doors watching the fire that had broken out, and not realising the awful danger they were in. Suddenly there was a deafening roar, a fountain of flaming debris was projected high into the air and this spread out like a fiery rose, dropping death and destruction over the whole district. The force of the explosion sent pieces of machinery, some weighing many tons, flying through the air with the result that the cottages and factory buildings that were not wrecked by the concussion, were crushed and battered by the hail of fragments that came raining down upon them.

Several streets of houses were converted into heaps of rubble in a second. Those that escaped total destruction stood up as mere skeletons among the wreckage.

The scene immediately after the explosion beggared description. The burning debris had started fires in many of the factories and mills round about, which became roaring furnaces as the night progressed. In all directions people who had escaped serious injury were picking themselves up in a dazed condition. Mothers were frantically looking about for their little ones, many of whom were buried in the ruins, while on the pavements were the bodies of pedestrians who had been struck as they were walking along.

In common with all other buildings, the Church of St. Barnabas suffered almost total destruction. The iron room adjoining the Church was being used for a children's gathering, and although the roof collapsed, not one of the children suffered serious injury. Their escape seemed so miraculous that the fact is recorded on a memorial tablet which has been erected in the temporary hut Church.

It would take a much larger volume than this to record all the happenings of that night. If a soldier home on leave from the battle front had wandered into the district he could have imagined that he was back in one of those ruined villages that were scattered about the firing line. As a spectacle, England will probably never see its equal. In all directions great buildings were blazing, fire engines and ambulances were dashing up from all parts of London, hundreds of volunteers were at work rescuing the injured and searching the ruins for bodies. Homeless people were wandering off to neighbouring districts where every available hall had been thrown open to give them shelter.

As the object of this book is to concentrate attention on the religious and social work carried on by the Priest-in-Charge and staff of St. Barnabas Church, West Silvertown. I cannot do better than give the account of the then Priest-in-Charge, written soon after the disaster, of the part played by the Church in dealing with the effects of the explosion.

The great explosion at West Silvertown occurred on Friday January 19th 1917, at about 7 p.m. At the time the Band of Hope children numbering between 60 and 70, were having their treat in the Parish Hall. Tea was finished, the tables cleared and games had been started when we received the warning that —'s Factory was on fire. Almost as soon as we had the warning the explosion occurred and the building collapsed on top of us. At first we seemed to be in total darkness but very soon (in what seemed to be a few seconds) fire had broken out in many parts of the neighbourhood and the whole place was lit up by the lurid glare. Fortunately none of our workers lost consciousness and all set to work at once to rescue the children. It is with deep gratitude to God that one is able to record that not one of our party (numbering over 70, including workers) was killed, nor were any very seriously injured. As soon as we were satisfied that all the children were rescued we were able to turn our attention elsewhere and very soon discovered how terrible and widespread the disaster was! The whole Parish was practically destroyed, and a much wider area very seriously affected. Within an hour help was arriving from all parts of London, and the work of rescue and attending the wounded was in full swing. It is impossible to touch upon the splendid work done in all quarters; we can only tell of that small portion centred at St. Barnabas.

We at once set to work in the Parsonage kitchen which was the least damaged of the rooms and most accessible. Bedding and rugs were laid on the floor for the sufferers, and it at once became the dressing station and clearing house for ambulance work in the immediate neighbourhood.

From Monday 22nd we found it necessary to provide food and warmth for the people, as many were returning to look after their furniture and recover what they could from their ruined homes. The dining room, study and kitchen was cleared and made as comfortable as possible, and for over a fortnight hot drinks and food were dispensed free of charge. The weather at that time was bitterly cold, and the house was continuously full of people who came for food and a warm. The Church Army was exceedingly good to us, giving funds and food to help in this work. Help was also forthcoming from the Corporation Distress Fund and private friends in the shape of money, food, coal, clothing and personal service.

The work of clothing was of next importance. Many had escaped with their lives, but with very little else. The clothes they were wearing at the time of the explosion were all they were able to rescue, and in most cases they were torn to shreds! We started a clothing depot at the North Woolwich School where we received many gifts of clothing, and were able to make people comfortable. The work of sorting the clothing and handing it out to those in need was undertaken by the staff of West Silvertown Council School. The number of cases they dealt with ran into thousands, and their work was beyond praise. This work was carried on long after the Central Depot was closed as we found it necessary to provide for our people when they recovered from their injuries and were discharged from hospital. We were also able to assist largely with the children and, provide that they should be suitably clothed when they went to various convalescent homes and the country school which was started at Swanley. Various gifts of money had to disbursed to tide people over temporary difficulties, and it is with gratitude to God that we are able to say that sufficient means were forthcoming to do so.

This is a very rough sketch of the work done at St. Barnabas, and does not in any way touch upon the work that was done so willingly and well by others. The clothing and feeding, etc., was done by voluntary help and gifts, amounting to £119 in money, and about £200 worth of clothing, sent from friends in all parts of the country.

Gratitude to our friends, and above all to our Heavenly Father for His mercy, has prompted this brief record by

WALTER G. FARLEY
Late Priest -in-Charge

PART III

The foregoing report enables me with ease to bring you, my readers, to the one reason for the existence of this book, which is, as I have already hinted, to enlist your sympathy and support for the work now being carried on by the present priest-in-charge (Rev. Wm. Chas. Bown).

Mr. Bown was appointed as Mr. Farley's successor shortly after the explosion, and took up his duties as soon as he possibly could. After reading the account of the havoc wrought by the explosion, it will need a vivid imagination to picture the tremendous uphill task Mr. Bown had in front of him, for although both the Church and congregation had disappeared, the latter gradually drifted back as the homes were rebuilt, but the former does not, alas, exist in a permanent form yet.

The first thing to be done then was to provide some accommodation for worship and a hut church was speedily erected on part of the site occupied by the old church, with a seating accommodation of 90. The accommodation soon proved to be insufficient and an extension was built and opened in the Autumn of 1918. The little hut church – with a seating accommodation of 250 for a district of over five thousand souls! To a man of Mr. Bown's energy and enthusiasm, this is a position not to be tolerated, and with the sanction of the Bishop, and the approval of the London-over-the-Border Fund, which is directly responsible for the 'Mission District of St. Barnabas', he is now making a great effort to secure funds to build a new permanent Church and Hall, which will not only be worthy of the One to whom they will be consecrated, but will also prove to be a real tower of strength to the people in the district. To realise the truth of this statement it must be understood that, with the exception of the ubiquitous public house, there is only one centre for social intercourse and that is a small Non-conformist chapel is also working under great difficulties. There is not even a penny picture theatre in the district!

Although undoubtedly the main effort should be concentrated on the erection of the permanent church and hall as rapidly as possible, it has been fully realized that the immediate needs of the people must not be neglected. To provide room for the various organizations connected with the Church and for social intercourse, part of the hut church had to be curtained off and used for this purpose, when not required for worship. At mid-day it was used as a Rest Hut for the many girl workers in the neighbouring factories who live out of the district, and each evening it was in use either by the Girl's Club, or the C.L.B. Cadets, the Girls V.A.D. Detachments, or for an occasional 'Social'.

All this social activity was found to interfere somewhat with the spiritual use of the building inasmuch that it robbed it of the 'atmosphere' that one finds in a church used solely for spiritual worship. The next step, therefore was to find new temporary quarters for the social organizations. A disused stable and loft were placed at Mr. Bown's disposal by one of his supporters and he soon made them as comfortable as conditions would permit. The stable was fitted up with gymnastic apparatus, and is now used by the Men's and Boy's clubs, while the Rest Room referred to has been transferred to the loft above, which is also used for club purposes.

The District for ecclesiastical reasons, has recently been enlarged by the addition of several rows of small houses situated on the either side of the Dock entrance. It is evident that the people of this locality would find it difficult to attend St. Barnabas Church, and it was therefore, decided to take the Church to them. A disused public house was purchased and fitted up as a Mission Hall, which will shortly be opened.

The most important point will be remembered in that the whole of the church work of the district is being carried on in temporary and most unsuitable buildings, quite inadequate for the purposes for which they are used. A glance at a few of the organizations connected with the church should show how badly a large well-equipped hall and institute are needed.

Two of the foremost organizations are the Church Lads' Brigade (affiliated to the King's Royal Rifle Corps) with its Junior Training Corps, and the Girls Junior V.A.D. Detachment. The Church Lads' Brigade is in full khaki uniform with regulation K.R.R. badges and buttons and is proud of the fact that it is affiliated to the 16th K.R.R. which was formed at the outbreak of war and was recruited entirely from old C.L.B. lads. The Girls V.A.D. Detachment is a junior organization recognised by the British Red Cross Society, and is composed of girls who are working during the day in the local offices and factories. They undergo regular training in First Aid and are gradually becoming a very useful detachment. There is also a flourishing Social Guild with about one hundred and fifty members, which is the means of bringing Communicants together at frequent intervals during the winter for pleasant social intercourse.

As it may be thought that the social side of the Church life is dwarfing the spiritual work, let it be pointed out at once that the reverse is rather the case. The Church, with its worshippers around the Altar, is the centre from which all other activities radiate. The number of acts of Communion from Easter to December 31st, 1918, amounted to eighteen hundred.

Although funds are so urgently needed for parochial purposes, Mr. Bown has always listened to urgent requests from organizations outside the district. Thus on Hospital Sunday, 1918, £20 was raised for the hospitals, and when the Church Army held their Flag Day, collectors from St. Barnabas made a collection totalling £37, a very creditable amount for an essentially working class district.

PART IV

Your interest has, I hope been sufficiently aroused to bring you to this point, for now I wish to make the personal appeal to you to help Mr. Bown and his staff in the uphill fight before them by sharing the financial responsibility. A sum of £10,000 is needed to build the new church and hall, of which £2,500 has already been subscribed. I make the appeal with a certain amount of confidence, as if you think the matter over, you will find that you are bound by several ties to the people in whose name this appeal is made. The tie of our common humanity is understood and the tie of Christian Brotherhood will be understood by all those who have been baptised, but there is another tie that binds you with equal strength, and that is the social and economic tie. From the time you rise in the morning to the time you retire at night you are enjoying the products of the factories in which our people work:- the piece of fragrant smelling soap which gives an added pleasure to your ablutions; the marmalade, jam or syrup on the breakfast table; the sugar in your coffee; that polished wood tray with the pretty grain; the soda used in the household; the chemical manures on the garden and in the conservatories, are all made or prepared by your brothers and sisters in Silvertown. Some of the largest flour mills in the country are also situated in the district, as well as large oil works, dye works and timber yards.

Surely you will agree with me that whatever you are able to send to the Church at Silvertown should not be looked on as a charitable dole, but rather as an acknowledgment of the ties that bind you to our people, and as they are spending their lives looking after your material welfare so you are sending your mite to be used for their spiritual and social welfare.

A.W.

A subscription form is attached and may be sent with donations to Rev. Wm. Chas. Bown, St. Barnabas' Clergy House, Eastwood Road, West Silvertown, E.16.

CHAPTER 9
ST LUKE'S CHURCH, CANNING TOWN

St. Luke's Parish, Victoria Docks
Parish Magazine, February 1917

MY DEAR PEOPLE,

My thoughts in this Monthly Paper must be on the appalling catastrophe which has just occurred at our very doors – in the very next parish.

Friday, January 19th will long be remembered as a black day in the year 1917. The terrible explosion and fires which occurred shortly before 7 p.m. were perhaps the most violent and awful England has ever experienced. Oh, what a sad thing is War, which permits such deadly and destructive explosives to be manufactured in the midst of a teeming population. Though the death roll is heavy – no one can say how heavy, yet it is a mercy it is not tenfold greater.

A visit to the immediate district is appalling. Hundreds of houses have been swept away, hundreds more are mere skeletons – little better than blackened walls. It is most pathetic to see on some of the remaining walls pictures still hanging. The Church of St. Barnabas and places of worship have been entirely destroyed, and demolition and destruction are everywhere.

It is a comfort to know that everything has been done that could be done to alleviate distress, and to provide food and shelter and clothing for the weary and the homeless.

Our own parish has suffered – has suffered awfully, but after this sad district we may be thankful we have escaped so lightly. Most of our damage arises through smashed windows, splintered wood-work, falling ceilings and the like. The Vicarage has come in for its share. There is scarcely a room with sound windows. The Church after the explosion was an awful scene. On that Friday night it looked as if it would be impossible to use it for some time. The beautiful stained windows were broken – some blown entirely out. Matching had fallen from the ceiling; doors were burst open and debris and broken glass were everywhere.

However, with willing workers and true zeal, Saturday was so splendidly utilized that we were able to hold the Weekday and Sunday Services as usual. Mr. Bastow and Mr. Hills worked like tro-jans in boarding up the windows to keep out, as far as possible, wind and weather; and they were well supported by some of the good women, by cleaning the Church.

The Schools have suffered greatly. One fear was the chimney stacks falling. Some were more than a foot out of the perpendicu-lar, and we feared they would fall and break through the roof. Early on the Monday, workmen started in taking two of them down, and we trust by this timely action we have saved the Schools from fur-ther heavier damage. The School houses have also suffered. In Mr. Witham's house alone no less than 19 panes of glass had to be put in. Great damage has also occurred to the Institute, besides broken windows, a large chimney stack has fallen which has damaged three roofs. The Mission Church too has suffered.

But I must not go on. We are living in anxious times, and just at present we seem surrounded by clouds and darkness....

Believe me, yours very sincerely

J.C. BUCKLEY

St. Luke's Parish, Victoria Docks
July 1917

THE GREAT EXPLOSION. The Treasury had made an offer of a grant of £160 towards the cost of damage done by the explosion to our St. Luke's Day Schools and School Houses. There is an idea abroad that the Treasury are making good all damages. This is not so outside West Silvertown. The Treasury repudiate legal liability, but state they are willing to make reasonable grants. We hope the grant of £160, offered to the Trustees of St. Luke's Schools, will be sufficient to cover known damage. Mr. Jacques, the Borough Architect and Surveyor, has acted on our behalf, and the work has been carried out by Mr. Noakes.

CHAPTER 10
THE STRATFORD EXPRESS

'It seemed as if some vast volcanic eruption had burst out in the locality in question. The whole heavens were lit in awful splendour.'

Stratford Express, 27 January 1917

The Stratford Express *reports are taken directly from editions dated 27 January, 3 February and 10 February 1917. The newspaper was published twice a week, on Wednesday and Saturday, with some reports repeated in each edition. Although the explosion occurred on Friday 19 January, it was not reported in the newspaper until Wednesday 24th. As the Saturday editions reprinted Wednesday's reports and included extra articles and a full editorial, only the Saturday editions are included.*

Newspapers printed during wartime are subject to censorship and the Stratford Express *was no exception; therefore Brunner Mond's is referred to throughout the text as 'a munitions factory' and Silvertown is 'the affected district'. A rare exception is where in one paragraph reference is made to the 'Mayor of West Ham'. Also no churches or schools are named and where it has been possible to identify them, their names have been added in square brackets. These are the only additions to the original text and we have included mis-spellings of names where they occur. For instance, in the first edition Dr Angel is spelt Dr Angell and Mr Geoffrey Wainwright's first name is also printed as Jeffrey. The most common spelling of the names of those killed in the explosion are included in the list of casualties at the end of this publication.*

SATURDAY 27 JANUARY 1917

Editorial Column

The great tragedy which has fallen on the people of East London this week has for the time being overshadowed every other question. Even the war has been forgotten for the time being, except in so far as it was realised that the explosion was but a side issue of the great convulsion which has rent Europe during the past two and half years. As to the cause of the explosion, we can only say that the Government has promised an inquiry, and in the interests of all concerned that inquiry should be as searching and complete as it is possible to make it. Obviously, it cannot be so complete as many would have wished, because some of those best able to speak have met their deaths, but the grim fact should not deter the government from making a determined effort to arrive at the cause of the fire and subsequent events. The explosion has brought home to the minds of the people of East London in a terrific manner the effect of the modern high explosive. The death roll is already very heavy, and the loss of property is almost incalculable. Scores and scores of homes have been wrecked; hundreds of people are homeless. The government have consented to take the full responsibility, and we sincerely hope that the working people who have had their little homes destroyed will be treated generously. The explosion took place as a result of the nation's wants at this critical time, and the nation should foot the bill fairly and without stint.

Amidst the sorrow and gloom occasioned by the disaster there are certain matters which should give heart even to those pessimists who tell us – or rather used to tell us that the heart of England is rotten. First and foremost, there is the heroic conduct of Dr. Angell whose body has at last been found amongst the ruins of the factory. Had he been a craven, he might possibly have escaped with his life, but, like a true English gentleman – knowing full well the potentialities of a fire at such a factory – he remained at the spot where he felt his duty to be. Much the same can be said of the gallant firemen whose heroism and devotion to duty are typical of a brigade never yet lacking in brave men. No men knew better than they the risks they ran, but they faced their duty with a calm but heroic determination. Alas! their actual work was hardly commenced before the explosion took place, and two of them —Vickers and Sell — met their deaths. Ready assistance was given to those who were injured or rendered homeless, men and women of all classes have given their services in an unstinted manner; the rich and poor alike have flocked to the aid of the poor sufferers of this great national tragedy. In due course these workers should be publicly thanked. This remark applies especially to the Mayor. With the able assistance of the Town Clerk he was, within an hour of the accident, making arrangements for the succour of the homeless, and but for him and the many noble men and women who collaborated with him, hundreds of women and children would have spent the night in the streets.

From the point of view of the borough in which the explosion occurred, the catastrophe must necessarily have an enormous effect. In the first place, it must be remembered that thousands of pounds' worth of property will be thrown out of rateable value, and this will naturally affect the yield of the rate. Again, there is the question of the thousands of children who for the time being are without school places.

We understand that the Board of Education are very sympathetic in the matter, and we sincerely hope that the fact of these children not being able to attend school will not affect the grant. The district has throughout the war responded nobly to every appeal made by the government. Now that it has been so severely stricken we hope the government will stand by the district, and help, rather than penalise it, on account of the awful calamity.

The Great Explosion

Dealing with Disaster – A Tour of the Stricken Area
Local Authorities' Meetings – Inquest Stories – Official Accounts

Following the great explosion, which was heard not only all over London and the Home Counties, on Friday evening, but in places as far away as the north of Cambridgeshire and Norfolk, the Press Bureau issued the following communication on Saturday morning:-

'The Ministry of Munitions regret to announce that an explosion occurred last evening at a munitions factory in the neighbourhood of London. It is feared that the explosion was attended by considerable loss of life and damage to property.'

On Saturday evening the following further report was issued.

About 7 o'clock last night a fire started at a factory in the East of London near the river, which was employed on refining explosives. Fortunately, a few minutes elapsed after the commencement of the fire before the explosion occurred, during which interval many of the operatives were able to escape from the factory. The explosion appears to have involved practically all the explosives in the factory, which was itself completely destroyed.

Fires were caused in neighbouring warehouses and factories, one of the largest of which was an important flour mill. The effects of the explosion were felt for a great distance; three rows of small houses in the immediate neighbourhood were practically demolished, and considerable damage was occasioned to other property.

An engine from the local fire station had reached the spot and was playing on the fire when the explosion occurred. The engine itself was destroyed, but fortunately only two of the firemen appear to have lost their lives.

The chief chemist of the factory and a number of other work people were killed by the explosion or buried in the ruins.

The chief chemist, Dr. Angell, whilst advising the operatives to seek safety, himself went to the fire and attempted to combat it. The

number of persons killed, either in the factory or in the neighbouring house, is not yet ascertained.

The casualties, however, owing to the warning which people
had by the outbreak of fire, are not nearly so heavy as was at first
anticipated. Up to the present between 30 and 40 bodies have been
recovered, and about a hundred persons are reported to have been
seriously injured.

Ample assistance was forthcoming from the London fire
brigades and a number of ambulances. The police and the municipal authorities have found temporary accommodation for those
whose homes have been damaged.

Certain firms have generously sent large subscriptions to the
Minister of Munitions with a view to their being used for the benefit of the sufferers, and the Local Government Board have undertaken, in conjunction with the local authority, to see to the
application of any funds raised in this way. In the meantime the
Minister has requested the Borough authorities to arrange for the
provision of immediate relief of those requiring it.

Owing to the effects of the explosion all communication with
other districts was broken off for a time. Local assistance was
immediately forthcoming, but, owing to the lack of communication, assistance from the Metropolitan Fire Brigade could not be
obtained immediately – the fire not being in the London Fire
Brigade area. Within half an hour, however, ample assistance was
afforded from all quarters.

We are further informed by the Ministry of Munitions that the
accident will make no practical difference to the output of
munitions.

The Minister, with the chief officers of the Explosives Supply
Department, visited the scene this morning, and every possible
effort is being made to deal promptly with the unfortunate effects
of the explosion. Both last night and this morning His Majesty the
King has made enquiries as to the extent of the damage and loss
of life, and has expressed his solicitude for the victims and their
families.

The Minister of Munitions, on behalf of the Government, has requested the local authorities and those in charge of the relief operations to convey his deep sympathy with all those affected.

On Tuesday it was announced that the Government has decided upon an enquiry into the cause of the explosion, and the following communication was given by the Press Bureau.

Claims Office Opened

An Office has been opened at Plaistow Library for the receipt of claims. The Town Council have granted the use of the magazine room on the ground floor for the purpose, and on Tuesday morning the work commenced. Over a dozen Government officials are at work in the office, and already a large number of claims have been received. Scores of personal applications have been made, in addition to which every post produces a fresh batch. Application forms should be addressed to:-

The Officer in Charge,
Ministry of Munitions Office,
Public Library,
North Street, Plaistow.

The department has very wisely issued a poster warning those who are making claims not to accept the assistance of unknown people in the making of claims, but rather to seek the advice and assistance of the officials.

Relief Subscriptions

On Tuesday the Ministry of Munitions also issued the following statement:-

'His Majesty the King has graciously contributed £250 towards the relief of the sufferers from the recent explosion. £100 has also been received from Her Majesty the Queen, and £100 from Her Majesty Queen Alexandra.'

On Wednesday the Ministry of Munitions announced that the Princess Royal had sent a contribution of £50 towards the relief of sufferers. The Lord Mayor had received several subscriptions for the relief of distress, including £525 from Messrs. William Cory & Son, Ltd.; £105 from Messrs. N.M. Rothschild & Sons; and £50 from Lord Moulton. These will be applied in dealing with exceptional cases, for which it will be difficult to use the National Relief Fund (which is being primarily drawn upon for the alleviation of the distressed).

Royal and Public Sympathy
Messages to the Mayor

During Tuesday the King made special enquiries at the various hospitals as to the condition of the injured, and a message of sympathy was received from Queen Alexandra.

The following message was received at Queen Mary's Hospital, Stratford, where 25 of the victims were taken in, all of whom but four, who died shortly after admission, are making satisfactory progress:

Their Majesties desire that the expression of their deep sympathy with them and their relatives may be conveyed to these patients, and they entertain the hope that their progress towards recovery may be well maintained.

At Poplar Hospital a similar message was received, and the Prime Minister with Mrs. Lloyd George, called on Sunday.

Major Parsons called at London Hospital on Tuesday with a message from the King and Queen.

The Mayor has received the following letter from the Minister of Munitions:-

Whitehall Place, S.W.
23rd January 1917.

Dear Mr. Mayor, –

I am sure that you will wish to make known in the locality the gracious messages and the generous donations in aid of the sufferers received from their Majesties the King and Queen and from H.M. Queen Alexandra, which are announced in Press today.

I enclose a copy of Queen Alexandra's telegram, and also of telegrams which I have received from the French Minister of Munitions, M. Loucheur; and from the General Hermonious, K.C.M.G., the chairman of the Russian Government Supply Committee in London. I also hope that you will make it known that I have received a warm expression of sympathy from General Orth, the head of the Belgian Mission in London.

Believe me,
Yours very truly,
CHRISTOPHER ADDISON

(Copy of Telegram)
Buckingham Palace,
January 22nd, 1917.

The Minister of Munitions, London.

Please convey my deepest sympathy and sorrow to all the sufferers by the terrible explosion and my great distress at the lamentable loss of life. I trust the injured are progressing as well as can be hoped for. I enclose £100 for the poor sufferers.

(signed) ALEXANDRA.

(Copy of Telegram)
SSS Paris Hors Comptes, Paris.
20187, 32, 21, 10H.50,
Sous Secrétaire Etat Fabrications

A Ministre Munitions, Londres.
825 I/FG permittez moi vous addresser toutes mes condoléances pour terrible accident de vendredi et laissez moi saluer avec vous victimes du devoir.

LOUCHEUR
20th January 1917

(Copy of Telegram)
Right Honourable Dr. Addison,
Minister of Munitions, Whitehall.

Please accept my warmest and deepest sympathy with you in the ministry in the great loss which you sustained by the explosion of the munitions factory. Believe me that the news has been received by us with the most heartfelt sympathy for you, and the deepest compassion for those who have perished.
(signed) HERMONIOUS,
Russian Government Committee.

The Casualties

Up to Tuesday evening it was estimated that the total death roll had been 69, with 72 seriously and 328 slightly injured.

No further bodies have been recovered, but a useful service which the committee has been able to perform has been the tracing of missing children. More than 100 little ones have been found and restored to their parents. For other children, including 7 in the hospitals, no claim has been made, and it is feared that these boys and girls have been left orphans by the explosion.

Dr Angel's Body Identified

One of the bodies recovered during the week end from the 'crater' formed by the explosion was on Wednesday identified as that of Dr. Andrea Angel, the heroic chemist who lost his life in attempting to fight the fire. Mrs. Angel and an official of the firm established the identity by the clothing.

A memorial service to the late Dr. Angel will be held at Christ Church, Oxford, on Sunday next. Dr. Angel had been Tutor in Chemistry to non-collegiate students there since 1903 till the outbreak of war. His teaching made a great impression on his pupils, and he was universally respected.

Firemen Heroes

Amongst the many brigades attending the fire were those of the various local bodies, two of whose firemen – Henry Vickers and Frederick Sell – gave up their lives in noble efforts to others; and five others – Firemen Chappell, Yabsley, and three of the name of Betts – were injured.

The Damage

Various estimates are current respecting the cost of the damage, One very rough estimate made by an insurance assessor places the cost at between £2,000,000 and £2,500,000.

Amongst the buildings damaged are many of the schools of the local education authority, 19 of which are actually closed.

Housing the Homeless
Rebuilding

Meanwhile, the homeless are being as well cared for as local kindness and organisation will permit. Some 200 of the refugees have been housed in a school, and another 400 are distributed among four other centres. Many gifts of clothing have been made to the committee which has been looking after the sufferers.

Forty-seven houses belonging to the Port of London Authority are being offered to those who have had their houses destroyed, and a number of houses at Woolwich.

The Prime Minister has requested Sir Alfred Mond, First Commissioner of Works, to proceed with the reconstruction and rebuilding of the damaged house property in the immediate area of the explosion. Work was started on Thursday morning on a formidable undertaking.

At the London Hospital on Thursday two of the four hitherto unidentified bodies were recognised as those of Alfred H. Prior and Mary Ann Betts.

Five Days After – A Tour of the District
Children's Wonderful Escape
By an 'Express' Special

'At the risk of seeming extravagant in the use of words,' writes our representative, 'I say unhesitatingly that language is inadequate to faithfully portray the scene as it exists today. When I set out on Wednesday to visit the scene of the great catastrophe I had, as everyone has, a mental picture formed from printed descriptions of what I should see.

'As soon as I reached the outskirts of the district I realised that my visualisation would require much amendment to bring it into conformity with the real picture. As I got more into the heart of the district I thought of "Gulliver in the land of the Lilliputians," and it seemed to me that the hand of the veritable Titan had been at work endeavouring to satiate an unconquerable lust for destruction. I saw streets of what, for lack of a more appropriate description, have been termed "wrecked houses". That, they certainly were; but it conveys no idea of the true state of affairs. They were demolished; not merely knocked down, but obliterated. It was simply as if they had never existed. Where previously a row of dwellings had stood there remained but a flattened heap of debris – not a collection of bricks and mortar and remnants of general household effects, but a conglomeration of rubbish seemingly cast promiscuously upon the ground. It is only reasonable to suppose that some sort of clearing up had been effected, for there remained nothing, except in a few instances, to indicate that the houses had ever contained the necessities of human occupation. Then there were those houses which had escaped total demolition, but had received a rude buffeting from the giant blast. Titan, armed with a mighty club, seemed to have struck indiscriminate blows in his attempt to batter the houses without wholly destroying them. Roofs had been lifted bodily from their positions and deposited in queer positions upon the side walls. Some had been ripped off entirely like the lid of a tin; others were blown to pieces, and flung away to alight where the attraction of Mother Earth overcame their borrowed power. The vagaries of the explosion added to the weird impression. In the remoter parts of the district where the damage was largely confined to the windows, these had suffered in remarkably divergent ways. Here the glass had simply vanished, leaving the frames clean as if prepared for the reception of new panes; there the frames had been carried bodily away; and, here again, the fronts of the houses had gone with them. Relics of lace curtains occasionally hid the interior of the houses from sight, but where the view was unobstructed the stairs could be seen canting over at an acute angle; the party walls stripped of their plaster and paper, revealing the bare lathes, like skeleton witnesses of the passing of a terrible power.

'At the place of the explosion itself the scene was ghastly. Standing by the side of the demolished fire station, I faced the actual spot where once had stood stately buildings, rearing aloft and humming with the busy throb of industrial life. Now all was changed; only a heap of grim and tortuous rubble and fragments remained to tell of the existence of the great factories. Steel girders, twisted and contorted by the insensate hand of Titan, and all the other scarred and grotesque remnants lay about in a state of indescribable confusion, pile upon pile. The terrible giant seemed to have worked himself into a condition of ungovernable fury, and to have used his awful powers in the endeavour to frustrate the pygmy handiwork of human beings. Only the pen of a Dante could convey the real impression of the scene to those who have not witnessed it. Apart from the knowledge of the appalling tragedy involved, the sight was physically nauseating. Acre upon acre of devastated buildings, shapeless, confused and hopeless. One vast heap of ruins, gruesome witnesses of the terrible power, followed by the man's best friend, but his worst enemy. In the middle of this horrible heap was a big hole, marking the exact spot where the explosion occurred. Hundreds of tons of earth had been forced out, to fall like a mantle of death upon the surrounding debris. The water that filled the cavity was still and sombre.

'Then I turned my attention to the fire station – or all that remained of it. Behind it was a row of houses, the former homes of those heroic fellows who went forth at the call of duty, in full knowledge of the fact that nothing but a miracle could save them from death and mutilation. Reference has made to these gallant men, but the full story of their bravery yet remains to be told. Living on the spot, they knew and appreciated the character of the factory, and cry that it was afire might well have daunted them. But, men in whom the blood flowed strongly, they hurled themselves at their grim task with quiet courage and determination to carry on, be the penalty what it might. There are eleven of them ordinarily, but they also serve a sub-station. Two men had gone to relieve their comrades there, so that there were but seven left. Bravely they essayed their task, but ere they could actually get to work the devastating blast hurled them down, killing two outright, and injuring all the others, two so seriously that their lives are despaired of. Henry Vickers and Frederick Sell gave up their lives in their noble efforts to save others, and their names will for ever be honoured in the annals of our fire fighters. Henry Chappell and Firemen Yabsley are seriously injured, and three firemen named Betts, including father and son, and another who is not a relative, but bears the same name, are also injured. Their courage was equal to that of the collective brigade, but their fortune – literally *la fortune de guerre* – was simply greater than that of their comrades.

'As if in sheer wantonness, the explosion left the tower of the station standing, a monument to the glory of the heroic men. The row of houses are but husks of their former completeness. The mighty force had denuded them of their windows and interior appointments, strewing broadcast, in pathetic disorder, the contents of the houses. From these dwellings the deathroll was heavy; not only did the men sacrifice themselves, but in many instances their families, too, paid the penalty of close proximity to the factory.

'A glorious feature of the appalling catastrophe is the spontaneous heroism displayed. In a hall adjoining a mission church [St Barnabas Church, Eastwood Road, Silvertown] in the vicinity a number of children – between 60 and 70 – were assembled for the enjoyment of a Band of Hope treat. They had finished tea, and were engaged in a game of kiss-in-the-ring when one of the helpers, Miss Griffiths, on going into the parsonage, noticed a flare in the sky, and told the Rev. W.G. Farley who was of the party. He went and looked and, on returning to the hall, told everyone to keep cool. Hardly had the words left his mouth when the explosion rent the air, flinging everyone to the ground. The building is of corrugated iron lined with matchboarding, and it appears to have caught some of the fury of the concussion. The walls parted outwards, and the apex of the roof fell to the floor, whilst the sides were to some extent held up by the walls. The place was plunged in darkness, and it was impossible to tell the extent of the damage. The glare from outside lit up the hall, and realising that the roof might totally collapse at any moment and bury the children, Miss Griffiths immediately ran to hold up the lowest part of the roof, supporting the weight to the best of her ability. Her helpers, including Sister Evans, Mrs. Burford, Mrs White and Mrs Nobbs, went to her assistance, and, other help being forthcoming, all the little ones were removed from the place. Of the total number only 3 were injured. One was removed to hospital, and the other two, after receiving medical attention, were taken home. There can be no doubt that the great presence of mind and courageous action of Miss Griffiths adverted a dire calamity. Viewing the ruins of the hall in daylight it seems certain that a marvellous intervention of providence had allowed the children to escape. It seemed impossible that so many could have been assembled and none killed.

'Incidentally, this is the place about which so many startling rumours were invented. The church immediately adjoining, a much more substantially built edifice, suffered greatly. The chancel was blown away, and it now presents the appearance of an uncompleted building. Next to the church is the parsonage, and this was badly smashed. Here I found Mr. Farley, with a wound on his nose, cheerfully ministering to the creature comforts of his neighbours, at the beck and call of everyone.

' "Tell me your story," I ventured to suggest, but he was far too busy to talk. He was wholeheartedly doing. "It is quite true about Miss Griffiths," he remarked as he dashed out into the street, intent upon doing everything possible to alleviate the sufferings of the bereaved and injured. Inside, a number of ladies were dispensing hot beverages, and the hospitality of the house was open to all.

'Out in the street the wind was blowing bitterly, and several small wood fires had started to warm and cheer those who stood about in little knots. I reluctantly took up my pilgrimage again, and met the Bishop of Barking making his way towards the parsonage. He, too, had been visiting the sphere of disaster, and was depressed by the sights. Years ago the Bishop laboured in that particular district, and pointing to a wrecked school building, he whimsically observed 'we built that'. He was in pursuit of the elusive Mr. Farley, and I left him.

'Thence I proceeded to the vicarage of another church [St Mark's Church, North Woolwich Road, Silvertown], and was cordially welcomed by the Rev. J. Smyth, the curate there. The vicar was out, doing his part of the herculian [*sic*] task that confronts everyone in the district. The church had suffered comparatively slight damage, though the ornamental cornices had been shorn away, and many of the windows smashed. Usually the choir assembles in the church on a Friday night for practice, but for some unknown reason this was not so on last Friday. The vicarage was also damaged by the explosion, but it had fortunately escaped the full fury.

' "I was away at the time," Mr. Smyth told me, "but on my way home I was informed that not a single house within a radius of two miles of the factory was left standing. You can easily imagine my relief on turning into — road, to see the tower of the church still erect. Those who were in the house at the time were told that there would certainly be another explosion, and were advised to run as hard as they could. However, they contented themselves with turning off the gas supply, and waiting, and fortunately the gloomy prophecy was not fulfilled. This end of the parish," he added, "has not suffered so severely. The explosion seemed to spend itself in the other direction." During our conversation Mr. Smyth told me of a curious incident. Four little fellows who had been put to bed were attracted to the window by the fire. The eldest one was frightened, and at his suggestion they completely enveloped themselves in the bedclothing. Immediately afterwards the explosion caused the roof of their home to collapse, but thanks to the protection of the bedclothing the falling debris did not injure them.

'Thence once more I returned to the origin of all the havoc. Some hundreds of yards from the factory stands a huge flour mill, a handsome "fire proof" building of reinforced concrete, on the side of the water. The interior was completely gutted, and a thin and mournful column of smoke still rose from the roof. A fire engine was pouring a heavy stream of water into the place and as if the depressing desolation of the picture needed a touch of Nature to complete it, festoons of icicles hung from the coping stones. The ground was deeply covered with sodden flour, whose virgin whiteness was stained to a sickly yellow.

'Adjoining warehouses measured their length upon the ground, their shells and contents burnt and charred beyond recognition. The stillness of the place, broken only by the monotonous throb of fire engines, seemed to eat into my very being, and I turned away sick at heart. All round the district huge chunks of steel plating, contorted as if in physical pain, lay where they had fallen, like sheets of paper scattered by a blast from the Titan's lungs. Here and there nondescript vehicles came along, laden with an odd assortment of tables and chairs, redeemed from the general wreckage.

'I then proceeded to the hall [Lees Hall, Barking Road, Canning Town] where the Emergency Committee has its headquarters, and there the atmosphere of death and desolation was left behind, giving place to comfort, warmth and light. The number of helpers, recruited from the ranks of social workers, the Salvation Army, soldiers, cadets, boy scouts, and many others, showed the general eagerness to assist to the utmost of human capacity. The two Hon. secretaries – Miss Towers and Mr. J.J. Harding – were busily engaged, but the latter found time for a brief chat. He related all that had been done for the sufferers, and what yet remained to be accomplished. Despite the absence of any public appeal, much was done by the sympathisers. Thousands of garments of all sorts had been sent to the hall, and parcels were coming in all the time.

' "Many of those who got away," Mr. Harding explained, "were only partially clad, and all are more or less in need of clothing. They come here and obtain a suitable outfit, selecting what best suits them. We have now opened six centres in the vicinity, where the people live and sleep. At each centre there is a trained nurse, and special constables guard the places through the night. This is the clearing house for everything, and no matter what the people want to know, they come here. A sub-committee has been today inspecting property, and have found what we hope will prove to be suitable accommodation for many of the families."

'Mr. Harding went on to speak of the generosity that had been displayed by the public, and he also said that those in need of money had been given it, though every reasonable precaution was taken to establish the bona fides of claimants. At one of the centres, he said, was a woman with twins only two weeks old, and five other children. All are doing well.

'Mr. Harding told some harrowing stories, only one of which I will record. One of the — firemen, having been treated at the hospital, set out to find his missing wife. He found her, poor fellow, in the mortuary at London Hospital. Three of his children were killed, but his cup of bitterness was not complete, for two others are missing.

'A less pathetic incident was also related by Mr. Harding. A little girl of eleven was escaping from her partly wrecked house, in the upper part of which was a Belgian woman with a week old baby. When outside she remembered the Belgians, and said to her sister "I am going back. You know the Belgians died for us." Unconscious of her heroism, the child returned to the house, and remained with the woman. The sequel, fortunately, is a happy one. The woman and her baby were rescued, and the little girl accompanied them to their temporary home.

' "I should like to peep into one of the centres," I suggested, and Mr. Harding readily complied, and escorted me to one nearby. Here again, cheerfulness was the predominating feature, and the grim tragedy through which they had passed seemed almost eliminated from the people's minds.

'The large hall was set apart as the mess-room, and in an antechamber I found the Rev. C.A. Duthie in charge of the commissariat. Hot dinners had been supplied, whilst stacks of bread and slabs of cake were in readiness for the final onslaught of the day. Mr. Duthie spoke in terms of appreciation of the generosity of local tradesmen and others.

'The classrooms had been turned into sleeping apartments, and I interviewed some of the junior occupants, who were in various stages of undress. They were happy in their novel surroundings, and those already in bed bade me a cheerful 'Good night'. I mentally dwelt on the charming irresponsibility of youth which allows so speedy a transition from tragedy to humour.

'All parties, all creeds, and all classes assist to the utmost of their power. The district has had that touch of nature which makes the whole world kin.'

Railwaymen's Sympathy

I am instructed by the members of Stratford No.1 Branch of the N.U.R. to send, through the medium of the Stratford Express, a vote of condolence in this their hour of bereavement to the relatives of the victims of the catastrophe. Our deepest sympathy goes out to them. We, as workers, realising the terrible anxiety and suffering that eventually follow in the trail of such a calamity, hope and trust that in this their hour of trial the utmost will be done to alleviate their suffering and comfort them. We also hope that the injured will soon be restored to health again. Furthermore, we hope that the government will see that, where possible, they will make good all the damage done by providing for the dependants that are left, providing every comfort for those who have been crippled, and by providing homes, etc., for those who have lost same.

E. Wenlock, Assistant Sec.

Dockers' Sympathy

The following is a copy of a resolution passed by the Executive Council of the Dock, Wharf, Riverside and General Workers Union at its meeting just concluded:-

East London Explosion

This Executive Council of the Dock, Wharf, Riverside and General Workers Union offers its condolence to the bereaved of those destroyed by the East London explosion, many of whom were members of the above Union.

This Executive is of the opinion that the manufacture of high explosives should in every case be isolated and not carried on in thickly populated districts.

We also regret the loss of resources to the country, and trust the workers employed at other factories will concentrate their efforts to prevent any diminution in total output.

We trust an immediate enquiry into the matter will be instituted, and that ample compensation will be provided to the relatives of the victims.

East Ham Council's Sympathy

Before the commencement of the business at East Ham Town Council on Tuesday evening the Mayor (Councillor R. Banks Martin) moved that a letter be forwarded to the Mayor of the borough in which the explosion occurred expressing profound sympathy with the sufferers, and also appreciation of what His Worship had done in relieving the distress.

The proposition was carried unanimously.

Independent Labour Party

The East London Federation passed the following resolution at their last meeting:-

'That this delegate meeting of the I.L.P. branches in East London offer their deepest sympathy to their fellow workers who have lost relatives or friends in the explosion and fire of last Friday, and to those who have unfortunately suffered injured they hope for a speedy and complete recovery. They further place on record their protest at explosives being produced, with the sanction of the authorities, in a manufacturing neighbourhood thickly populated by the working classes.'

Story of the Explosion

In two short sentences the government on Saturday morning announced to the people of London the fact that an explosion had occurred at a munition factory. It was not till late on Saturday afternoon that the government issued, or allowed to be issued, any details of the terrible calamity of the previous evening.

On Friday evening, just before 7 o'clock, those who were busy in shops and offices had their first intimation that something was wrong by the partial failure of the electric light. It was, however, only momentary, but immediately there was a sound of a stupendous explosion. The firing of a heavy gun is as nothing compared with the noise. The report was heard throughout London and Greater London, and windows, pictures and ornaments miles away from the scene of the accident were smashed by the violent displacement of the air.

The explosion was followed by a scene which will never be forgotten by those who witnessed it. It seemed as if some vast volcanic eruption had burst out in the locality in question. The whole heavens were lit in awful splendour. A firy [sic] glow seemed to have come over the dark and miserable January evening, and objects which a few minutes before had been blotted out in the intense darkness were silhouetted against the sky.

The awful illumination lasted in its eerie glory only a few seconds. Gradually it died away, but down by the river rose a huge column of flame, which told thousands that the explosion had been followed by fire and havoc the like of which has never been known in these parts.

Throughout the night the blaze came from this particular locality. Miles away from the spot trees and houses were clearly defined
against the red background in a strange but awful manner. Fire
engines and fire apparatus were brought from all parts to combat
the flames, but the conflagration continued, and it was not till
Sunday afternoon that it finally subdued. One of the buildings
which gave the firemen the greatest trouble was a neighbouring
flour mill, which has been practically gutted by the fire. Immense
volumes of water were poured into it before the flames were
overcome.

How the fire started will probably never be known, but at any
rate firemen were at work before the explosion occurred. Of this
gallant band of firemen who were first on the spot two were immediately killed by the explosion and the engine badly damaged. The
chief chemist at the works, Dr. Angell, also met his death in heroic
manner. He urged the employees to seek safety, but for his own part
stopped to assist in quelling the fire, and in so doing lost his life. The
deceased gentleman was only 40 years of age. Educated at Exeter
Grammar School and Christ Church, Oxford, he took a first class
in chemistry in 1899, graduated M.A. in 1903, and took his B.Sc.
degree three years later. He was lecturer in natural science at
Brasenose College.

One of the workers employed in the factory made the following
statement to a press representative: 'There were not more than 40
people on the premises, the day shift having gone. About 35 of
these were on the high explosive plant, the rest being in the offices
or elsewhere. I was at work in the office when I heard women
shrieking. I came down to the door and saw the high explosive
building thoroughly afire. Somehow, providentially, I was able to
get away without a scratch, though others going along the road
were knocked down beside me by flying missiles hurled in all
directions by the explosion. The force of the explosion seemed to
take a curious zig zag course, and it must have missed me, though I
could not have been more than 200 yards away. My first thought,
when I saw the whole plant aflame, was "This is the end of all

things for me". All I am clearly conscious of was a rain of heavy things falling continually in front of me. I know that six of us managed to get out safely.'

Soon after the catastrophe occurred all kinds of agencies were at work. Large numbers of firemen, special constables, soldiers, nurses and ambulance people from all parts of London were hurried to the scene, and everything possible was done for the injured and homeless. Great assistance was rendered by the Salvation Army, the Y.M.C.A., and other agencies. The Y.M.C.A. authorities sent vans loaded with food and hot drinks, so that those who had to remain on the scene at work should be supplied with food.

On Saturday the Mayor and several members of the Council were present, and the Mayor gave orders that everything necessary should be done to alleviate the suffering of the homeless people. They were housed and fed at various public buildings and church halls in another part of the locality. The Minister of Munitions also visited the scene of the disaster on Saturday morning, and on Sunday the Prime Minister, accompanied by Mrs. Lloyd George and some of the members of his family, also went there. The Prime Minister was also shown the remains of the factory and the other buildings involved, and was greatly touched by the sight of the wrecked homes of the former residents of the locality.

After the Disaster – Scenes of Ruin and Desolation

A visit to the scene after the explosion was sufficient to give anybody an idea of the terrific nature of the calamity. It is not too much to say that the whole aspect of this busy manufacturing centre has been entirely changed. Where the munition works once stood there remains nothing but a great heap of bricks, rubbish and ironwork, twisted into strange shapes by the fire and explosion. In the main road lay a huge mass of iron, which at one time was a powerful boiler. It is said to have weighed 15 tons, but it was wrenched from its place when the explosion took place and dropped in the roadway. Here it had to remain until Monday morning, when a large body of soldiers, by means of a windlass, managed to remove it to the side of the road.

Close to the scene of the explosion is – or rather was – the local sub fire station. The place has been literally demolished, and all that now remains of it is the high tower which the firemen used for practice purposes and for the drying and mending of the hose. Everything in the house appears to have been demolished, and the piano stands in a heap of rubbish with the front portion torn off, leaving the wires bare. Near to it is a huge piece of iron, and it seems as if this must have fallen on the building.

The official account states that 'three rows of small houses in the immediate neighbourhood were practically demolished, and considerable damage was done to other property'. The statement hardly conveys a full idea of the damage that has been done. Dwelling houses, factories, and even the barges moored in the vicinity have been damaged, in some cases in such a way that were it not for the tragedy of the whole thing it would be laughable. For instance, a well known member of the local authority on Saturday morning found a horse lying dead. It had been killed by a mass of falling metal, but in the yard close to the carcase there was a hen still sitting quietly on her eggs.

The one great blessing about the whole thing is that the catastrophe did not happen three or four hours later, when the people were in their beds. There can be little doubt that the casualties would have been infinitely greater had it not been that the people in the lower parts of the houses were sheltered to a large extent from the flying missiles by the roofs. Even now a large piece of an iron girder is suspended on the upper walls of one of these small houses. The roof was smashed in, but the girder remains lodged on the wall.

Men and women who live in the district and were at home when the explosion took place describe the experiences as terrifying in the extreme. Bricks, masonry, and pieces of ironwork fell in all directions, and many people were injured in this way.

On Monday morning many of the people who had been cared for in various ways during the meantime made their way back to their homes in order to save some of the more cherished portions of their furniture. The homes of many of these poor people have been completely destroyed, and where a few poor articles of furniture have been saved from the wreckage they have been carried into the streets with the idea of having them removed at a later period.

In one of the roads, some hundreds of yards form the munitions factory, an employee in a soap factory was leaning disconsolately on the front gate. His home was typical of many others in the district, except for the fact that he and his wife and children had a miraculous escape from sudden death. In order that she might go out with her husband on Saturday afternoon, the wife had done most of her house cleaning on Friday, and was just finishing when the explosion occurred. A mass of ironwork – apparently a piece of girder – which must have weighed several hundredweight came through the roof and fell on the iron bedstead. The bedstead was doubled up, but curiously enough the ironwork did not come through to the room below where the members of the family were sitting. Every window in the house was blown out by the force of the explosion and the roof ripped off. Practically all the furniture was destroyed. In the front bedroom a picture about a foot square was lifted from the wall and driven cornerways into the lath and plaster of the wall with such force that it could not be removed. The picture was not broken though, and although the majority of the furniture in the room was smashed to pieces, the glass and china ornaments on the mantelpiece were not damaged in any way. Except for the fact that the man's wife was thrown down by the force of the explosion and bruised, all the inmates of the house escaped without injury. 'I shall never get another home, I suppose,' said the man, 'but I must be thankful that we are all alive'.

A short way from this man's house a church and church hall [stood]. In the latter place a number of the children were being given a treat. The windows of the church, the vicarage, and the hall were blown in all directions, but so far as can be gathered none of the children were injured seriously.

In spite of the havoc and desolation all round, the people in the district have not lost all hope. The number of shops down there is not great, but early on Monday morning the tradesmen were rearranging their scattered stores, and, though the shops were windowless, and there was much to depress the shopkeepers, they had notices outside their premises 'Business as usual.'

As we have already said, the damage to life and property in the near zone of the district has been great, and the remark applies to a lesser degree to the district which may generally be called the outer zone. Where the premises face south great damage has been done to property. The broken windows in this area can only be numbered by thousands, and in some cases, not only have the windows been broken, but the window frames have been blown into the rooms and smashed the furniture.

Aiding the Homeless

The task of helping those rendered homeless by the disaster was at once organised. At the time the catastrophe occurred the Mayor of West Ham was waiting to preside over a local meeting, and on receiving a summons from the Town Clerk he proceeded to the Town Hall. He was soon at the scene of the accident, and took an active part in providing shelter for the homeless. A central relief station was opened at a hall under the auspices of a Ladies Settlement [Canning Town Women's Settlement, Lees Hall, Barking Road, Canning Town], the residents of which worked with a devotion which was most praiseworthy. A card-index system was speedily organised, which enabled separated members of families to become re-united.

Other relief work was carried out at various centres, under the charge of Anglicans, Roman Catholics and Baptists.

The Minister of Munitions authorised the municipal authorities to expend what was necessary in providing food for the sufferers.

On Saturday morning a committee was formed by the Mayor to deal with the relief of the distressed. Although no fund has been opened, money has been forwarded to the town hall for this purpose.

The Emergency Committee called together by the Mayor of West Ham to deal with the distress caused by the explosion wishes it to be understood by the general public that no person is authorised to collect money on its behalf.

No subscriptions of money from the general public are required. The Ministry of Munitions and the Local Government Board have taken over the care of the families rendered homeless.

All relief will be issued by the Emergency Committee, who have about five hundred people to accommodate and feed. Schools and local halls are being used for the purpose.

Red Cross and ambulance workers flocked into the district from all parts of London, and rendered yeoman service.

A word of special praise should be accorded to the work of the Salvation Army. Their work was carried out under the auspices of Mrs Bramwell Booth, the wife of the General. Besides providing material comfort for the sufferers, the officers did much to cheer the afflicted. At the inquest on Monday the Army provided refreshments for the witnesses in attendance, and a lady officer gently led forward each of the women who had to give evidence. Food depots were also opened in the immediate vicinity of the catastrophe.

The Y.M.C.A., ever to the fore, sent down provision vans with refreshments for the soldiers at work on the scene.

Firemen's Gallantry

The Superintendent of the Fire Brigade paid a high tribute to the gallantry of the of the officers at the branch station wrecked by the explosion. Two of the firemen were killed and several injured.

Station-officer Betts, who was injured, is in sad distress at no news of his wife. She was home with her two daughters and a son at the time. The children were rescued, but there is no trace of their mother. Mr. Betts, after receiving treatment at the hospital, left on Monday to undertake a search for his wife.

One of the men killed leaves a widow and daughter at home, and has a son at the front. He has been a fireman for 23 years.

The other fireman killed was 11 years with the Corporation. His daughter, who was 17, and had recently won a scholarship at a local secondary school, was also killed. This officer leaves several children. Another officer – there were seven at the station – found that his wife and three children had been injured.

Another of his children was killed, and there is still another missing. An officer from this station who was seriously hurt remains in hospital. His wife and child were injured. All the firemen lived in a row of houses adjoining the wrecked station. The firemen, of course, were aware of the risk from explosion, but never flinched.

The station officer's words of warning, 'You know what this place is; now be careful,' had scarcely left his lips when the explosion occurred.

A Looter Sentenced – Conductor's Despicable Conduct

At West Ham Police Court on Monday (22nd Jan), before the Stipendary, R. A. Gillespie, Esq., John Podesta, 27, a bus conductor of Chester-buildings, Loman-grove, Camberwell, was charged with stealing cigarettes, coffee, etc., from the property of Ann McCready.

Constable Tindale 688A, said he was on special duty at noon on Saturday in a street which had been wrecked by the explosion.

The Clerk: 'You were on duty to prevent looting?' – 'I was looking out for it, but was on general duty.'

Witness added that he saw someone in the shop, and found the prisoner there with several articles in his hand. Asked what he was doing, he said 'I live here.' Afterwards he said he was 'just having a look round.' Witness noticed a box of cigarettes under his coat, and he arrested him. On searching him at Canning Town Police Station witness found a quantity of cigarettes, a box of cigars, a box of beef cubes, boot polish, fancy soap, a purse, bloodstained spectacles, and other articles.

The Clerk: 'Was it a shop where they sold cigarettes?' – 'Yes; it was a small general shop.' 'And the owner was badly injured?' – 'I heard it afterwards.'

In reply to further questions, witness said the prisoner was in charge of one of the commandeered buses used to convey soldiers to the scene of the disaster to prevent looting. Mrs. McCready, who appeared very distressed, said she kept a general shop, but it was wrecked by the explosion, and her husband was badly injured. The articles found in the prisoner's possession she identified as her property. The spectacles became bloodstained through her attending to her husband. Prisoner said he was a time expired soldier, having served in India and Africa. He was re-called to the Colours at the outbreak of war and took part in battle of Mons. He was subsequently discharged from the Army on account of epilepsy. When he arrived on the scene on Saturday he saw a number of soldiers picking things up, and did the same, but he did not know what for. 'I have not a stain on my character,' he added.

The Clerk: 'Don't be too sure about that because you have been charged before.'

Prisoner: 'I have never been charged before.'

'Weren't you charged at Marlboro'-street?' – 'I might have been as a child.'

'You were charged for unlawful possession and bound over. If you deny it, you will be remanded. Now do you deny it?' – 'No, if you have got it down there it must be so.'

The Magistrate: 'It is a cowardly and mean thing to do to people after they have had their houses wrecked, especially to rob a poor woman of her spectacles. You will be sentenced to three months hard labour.' Prisoner appeared staggered by the sentence. The Magistrate commended the constable who effected the prisoner's arrest.

Alleged Juvenile Looters

At West Ham Children's Court on Friday morning (24th Jan.), Harry Croxson, 13, of 28, Scott-street, Canning Town and Thomas Jacques, 12, of 93, Scott-street, schoolboys, were charged with the unlawful possession of drawing compasses and various articles of clothing. The Clerk said the articles were looted from a house damaged by the explosion.

Constable Challis 128K, said he saw a number of boys in the district pulling a barrow. When he approached, the others ran off but the prisoners were roped to the barrow and could not get away. In an old cap in the barrow were a number of drawing compasses and a further search revealed the other articles. The compasses had been stolen from a home the occupiers of which were injured and are now in hospital.

Prisoners who denied all knowledge of what was in the barrow, were remanded with a view to being charged with theft.

The Inquest Opened

The inquest on the bodies of the victims were opened on Monday afternoon, when formal evidence of identification was taken, and the inquiry adjourned for a fortnight.

After being sworn in early in the afternoon, the jury were taken to a neighbouring hospital, where three bodies were seen. Another hospital was visited, and the jury inspected several bodies in improvised mortuaries in schools and other buildings. In one, which is the immediate vicinity of the disaster, were seven unidentified and unrecognisable bodies, together with a dozen other victims who had been identified. In all the jury viewed about 53 bodies, and visited the scene of the explosion, driving round the district in a private motor bus. The coroner, who has expert knowledge of the district, explained the details to them of the various factories which had been destroyed. Afterwards the jury re-assembled at another hall, where there was a large number of witnesses and others. The Mayor, wearing his chain of office, occupied a seat next to the Coroner; and Lord Claud Hamilton represented the G.E.R. Co.

The Coroner, in opening the proceedings, remarked that the borough in general, and the district where the explosion occurred in particular were proud of the part which its inhabitants had played in the war. They had taken the loss of their gallant sons with calm fortitude. This disastrous calamity had brought the horrors of the field of battle into their midst, where those who remained at home were doing their share so splendidly. Words could be of no avail, but before commencing their mournful task that afternoon he felt he must express on the jury's behalf and his own, heartfelt sympathy with the relatives of the victims, and those who were injured in this disaster.

The Mayor stated that he had received a message from the King and Queen, offering their profound sympathy with friends and relatives of the killed and injured.

On behalf of the council of the borough he (the Mayor) desired to express the deepest sympathy of all with the friends and relatives of those who had been smitten down by this catastrophe. As the chief citizen of the borough he did all he possibly could on Friday night, with the aid of others, to house and feed those who were rendered homeless. Up to the present time, so far as he had been able to gather, every homeless man, woman and child had been provided food and shelter. That was as far as they had been able to go. Numbers were still coming in. They had made a certain hall the headquarters and centre of information, where anyone who applied would be assisted to find food and shelter. When the council met the following night they would take over full control, and provide for those who were homeless. It had been a very difficult task since Friday night. So far they had dealt with 600 homeless men, women and children, and he thought it quite possible that by the end of that day the number would be nearer 1,000. People had been taken temporarily into the homes of their relatives and friends, but that, of course, could not continue. So far as the distress was concerned, from what he could gather, definite arrangements would be made to house those who had been displaced, and for his own part he could assure them that no stone would be left unturned to help them.

Mr. Oxley, representing the Local Government Board, said he had been instructed to express the sincere sympathy of the Board with those who had suffered in this calamity. At the request of the Prime Minister and the Minister of Munitions, the Local Government Board had undertaken to supervise and assist in every possible way those who had suffered by the calamity. It was impossible to say more at present, but he could assure them that everything that possibly could be done would be done. A letter on the subject had been addressed to the Mayor of the Borough, who had been asked to make all immediate arrangements.

Lord Claud Hamilton said, as one intimately connected with that district through the Great Eastern Railway, he thought he would like to come down and express the heartfelt sympathy of the Company in the terrible calamity which had fallen upon them. He could assure them of their sincere sympathy with the relatives of those who had been lost.

A representative of the Ministry of Munitions said he desired to associate the Ministry with all that had been said, and to express sincere sympathy with all those who had suffered. The work had been carried on at the factory on behalf of the Ministry of Munitions, and all proper claims for damage and injury to persons would be met by the Ministry, and announcements would shortly be made, through the press, as to dealing with those claims. A Special Claims office would be opened in the borough, where small claims would be met on the spot, and big claims dealt with otherwise. All claimants would receive every assistance.

The secretary of the Company owning the munition factory at which the explosion occurred said he had been instructed to express the deep regret and sincere sympathy which they felt for all their friends and employees who had suffered injury or damage. The loss of so many of their staff and workmen was a deep personal blow to them, and they wished to express sincere sympathy with their relatives and friends, the company hoped the knowledge that they died doing their duty, no less than the men in France, would be some consolation to the survivors. Instances of bravery revealed by those who had escaped were truly remarkable, and had impressed everyone in the country.

They knew the appalling danger which combating of the flames involved; the conduct of the firemen; the watchman who ran back to open the gate for the firemen to get in, and the employees to get out; and the supreme courage of Dr. Angell, were instances of that bravery. So far as the work people were concerned their claims would be dealt with by the company in the fullest and most generous manner. Dr. Angell was not a permanent member of the company's staff; he joined shortly after the outbreak of war to assist in the work which they were asked by the Ministry of Munitions to undertake, and the company would make the care of his wife their first consideration.

Heartrending Stories

The coroner then proceeded to take evidence of identification of the bodies after which he adjourned the proceedings for a fortnight, remarking that in the meantime it might be necessary to trouble the jury again for the purpose of identification of other bodies.

The first witness was that of the licensee of a public house, who identified the body of his manager, age 36, who was found on the premises by the police.

A City fruit salesman identified the body of his grandfather, age 57.

A labourer living near the scene of the explosion identified the body of his son, age 8.

A working man deposed to finding the body of his daughter, aged 21 outside his house. Unfortunately he had lost another daughter, aged 23.

A labourer identified the bodies of his son and two daughters.

The body of a Liverpool plumber, aged 30, was identified by his landlady.

A son-in-law described how he found the body of his father-in-law, an engineer's fitter, aged 53, lying in a butcher's shop.

A hawker described how his brother-in-law, also a hawker, went out with a van in the morning and was found dead.

A labourer said he discovered the body of his wife in the office in the factory where she was employed.

A roller man identified the body of his wife and eleven-month-old daughter.

The bodies of the two local firemen were identified by a son and brother respectively.

A lady who had her arm bandaged said she was having her tea with her husband when they saw the light. He advised her to leave the house. She did so, but her husband was buried in the debris of the house, which collapsed. The body was not recovered until that morning.

A mill hand identified the body of his wife, aged 32, which he saw in a mortuary. At another mortuary he recognised his son, aged 13, and found a little daughter, aged 10, amongst the ruins of his house.

In all, evidence of identification in 36 cases was taken.

At the close of the proceedings the foreman of the jury expressed their sympathy with the relatives of the deceased.

The Coroner stated that all property found on the bodies was now in the hands of the police, and would be handed to the relatives.

London Hospital Inquests

At the London Hospital on Monday morning the inquest was opened on 15 of the victims. Only 11 were identified. Four died at Poplar, and the remainder at the London Hospital. Among the bodies were those of 5 women.

The first case was that of George William Galloway, who, Mr. Scott (representing the Great Eastern Railway) said, was an engine driver on the line.

Ann Galloway the widow gave evidence in tones scarcely audible. Her husband, she stated, left home at 4.30 on Friday afternoon to go to his engine.

The Coroner: 'About 10 o'clock the same evening you heard that he had been injured by the explosion?' – 'Yes.'

'You did not know for some time where he was?' – 'No.'

'And you found him at 4 o'clock on Saturday afternoon at the Sick Asylum?' – 'Yes.'

'Did he say what happened?' – 'He said there was a loud roar and he remembered nothing more. He could give no particulars, as he was not really conscious. At half past eight on Sunday morning I heard that he was dead.'

'Was he on the engine at the time of the explosion?' – 'I do not know.'

In the case of Winifred Snell, 15, Harold Snell, a clerk, identified the body as that of his sister. She had been carried out by a fireman. Their father was a fireman.

At 7.30 he saw his sister being carried from a field to the edge of the pavement. He lived at the fire station.

'Is that the fire station which has been so much damaged?' – 'Yes.'

'Was it blown to pieces?' – 'Yes.'

'Your father has lost his life?' – 'He was killed at the time of the explosion when working there.'

He found the fire station blown down. He assisted to lay his sister on a mattress, and she died there. 'She was found in a field adjoining the fire station with her back broken', he added.

'You think that she was blown there by the explosion?' – 'I have not formed an opinion. I have another brother in another hospital injured. My mother is in hospital suffering from shock, and another brother is in hospital.'

Medical evidence showed that the girl had a wound on the right hip and bruising of the spine. There was a fracture of the pelvis; something had evidently struck her violently.

The Coroner: 'We only know that she was found in a field. She might have blown against something.'

Work of the Invalid Kitchens of London

Almost the first of the distributing agencies to come to the relief of the East End inhabitants rendered temporarily homeless by the explosion was the Invalid Kitchens of London. As soon as the magnitude of the disaster was known this organisation, which has 17 branches throughout the East End of London, undertook to feed the stranded refugees, and has fed several thousand during the past week. In this connection there was a somewhat pathetic incident when a motor car, which is being used by the workers at the Kitchens in order to cover the ground between one feeding centre and another more quickly, was lent for a short time to a working man and his wife who were anxious to go and inspect the extent of the damage to their home, and, if possible, to rescue some of their domestic treasures. On their arrival at the spot, which is within a stone's throw of the destroyed factory, the couple found, unfortunately, that very little remained of their home, but, to their surprise, 12 hens which they kept in a pen at the back of their premises had escaped unscathed. A business transaction was at once effected, and the hens were sold at a good profit to the Invalid Kitchens of London, and have since formed a substantial addition to dinners supplied to the refugees from that organisation.

Queen Mary's Hospital
Thanks to Helpers

Will you allow me, through the columns of your valuable paper to express our most sincere thanks to all those ladies and gentlemen who so kindly volunteered their assistance in dealing with the admission of cases from the East End explosion on Friday last?

Their help was very gratefully appreciated, and facilitated the treatment of the poor sufferers.

A.W. SCRIVENER
Secretary.

The Council Meeting
What Has Been Done for the Homeless – Royal Sympathy
Local Firemen's Supreme Sacrifice

When the Town Council met on Tuesday practically the whole evening was spent in dealing with matters arising out of the great catastrophe. No other public business was discussed, and if any member took objection to any recommendation of a committee the clause in question was referred to the next meeting of the Council. Prior to the public meeting of the Council a private sitting was held to deal with the same matter.

When the public meeting of the Council commenced, the Town Clerk at once proceeded to read messages received. The first was from the King and Queen, expressing their profound sympathy with the victims of the disaster, and enquiring as to the condition of the injured.

Alderman Thorne, M.P., wrote as follows: 'I much regret that I am obliged to be absent from the Council meeting on Tuesday. Accustomed as we are to events in their more sombre phase, I feel sure that the Council will meet in a deeper atmosphere of sorrow than has ever before shadowed our deliberations. Let me at once express my profound sympathy with the bereaved, with the injured and with the people whose small, but treasured homes have been destroyed or damaged by this great calamity. You, Mr. Mayor, and the Town Clerk of the Borough deserve hearty commendation for the energetic manner in which you immediately set to work to relieve the suffering, and the grateful thanks of the people will go to the — House Workers and the clergy for their untiring efforts of succour. I place myself entirely at the disposal of those who may be appointed to organise the work of relief, and will gladly help in every way possible. In conclusion, I refer to the bravery displayed by our firemen, Dr. Angel, and others whose names are not publicly known. In the face of certain death these heroes remained at the post of duty, doing their best to save others, and I trust that their courage and devotion will remain immortalised in the records of public life in the Borough.'

The Deputy-Mayor wrote apologising for non-attendance, and stating that a conference representing two and a quarter millions of workers sent their sincere sympathy with the relatives of those killed and injured.

The Belgian Minister sent a message deeply regretting the disaster, and conveying his heartfelt sympathy.

The Bishop of Chelmsford wrote in similar terms, and offering assistance.

A letter was received from the National Fire Brigade Union Executive stating that they learned with deep regret of the terrible calamity, and sympathising with the victims and their relatives.

On behalf of 750 fire brigades throughout the country they expressed their heartfelt sorrow for the relatives of their two brave confrères in the fire service who had so nobly sacrificed their lives for King and country and for the safety of the inhabitants of the district.

The Town Clerk stated that he had also received a large number of letters and messages from members of the public, and he was sorry he had been unable to keep records of them all.

Alderman Moore-Smith suggested that the Mayor, on behalf of the Council, should reply to all the letters expressing their appreciation of the sympathy and offers of help and that the letters themselves be entered on the minutes. Alderman Davis seconded; and this was agreed to.

The Town Clerk presented an interim report of the Emergency Committee. The Mayor, he said, called a meeting at a certain hall on Saturday, where during the previous night a large number of homeless people had been accommodated. Their numbers increased very rapidly, and an Emergency Committee was formed to deal with the situation. The Town Clerk proceeded to read the names of the Committee, and said the hall had been placed at their disposal, and the Committee had met daily. Offers of help had been received from various quarters, and the Committee arranged for the homeless people to be accommodated at various halls attached to the places of worship and other institutions in the district. The total number thus accommodated was 565 and they had been provided with food and clothing. There had been no public appeal, but about £160 had been sent in, besides a quantity of food and clothing. The Committee had been empowered to make grants of money in cases of urgent necessity. A bureau of information had been formed, lists of killed and injured published, and every assistance given to enable people to trace their relatives. The Committee had laid down certain recommendations, among which were the following: Every effort should be made to accommodate the homeless in the Borough itself (Hear, hear). There were unoccupied houses in the garden suburb of the Port of London Authority, and also a number of unoccupied shops which could be utilised. These should be commandeered, and no person should be removed from the borough until this had been done. Persons of the same family should not be separated from each other. Every facility should be granted to enable people to remove their effects from the wrecked homes to the new quarters. Any suggestion to remove people to work-houses or similar institutions would be strongly resented (Hear, hear). The scale of relief should be generous and at least equal to the new scale of Army Separation Allowances. These views had been represented to Lord Rhondda.

The Mayor said he desired, on behalf of the Council, to move a vote of condolence with the people who had suffered bereavement and, as far as possible, it should be conveyed to the relatives of all who had been killed.

This was carried in silence, the members standing.

The Mayor went on to say that, as far as the Emergency Committee's report went, it was very good, but it would not convey an idea of one quarter of the work done by them. He would like to give his own experiences. On Friday evening he left the Tribunal to take a meeting on the War Loan at the Conference Hall. He saw the flare in the sky, and a couple of minutes later heard the explosion.

He returned to the town hall, where some confusion reigned for a few minutes. A message was received from the Public Hall saying that the people were asking for admission there. He and the Town Clerk proceeded to the spot as soon as possible, and found about a hundred people already assembled.

The large hall was very much damaged by the broken glass, but whilst they were considering how best they could deal with the people a message was received from another hall, saying that if they could be of service in taking people in and feeding them they would be glad to do so. Eventually a very large crowd assembled there, and provisions were obtained for them. He and other members of the Council remained there most of the night. An Institute was opened and the men were transferred there, the women and children remaining at the hall, which had been opened continuously ever since. In the early morning of Saturday he and Alderman Thorne went through the district, and there met Dr. Addison, the Minister of Munitions. He (the Mayor) had a talk with him, and was satisfied that it was quite unnecessary to make any public appeal, and that was the chief ground for there being no such appeal. The Emergency Committee and the lady workers helped wonderfully, and, so far as he was aware, there had been no case of hunger, and no one had been left unhoused. Only those who had watched the work being done would be able to credit it. They decided to seek for other institutions, and by Saturday night they had other places going. An extraordinary number of helpers came along on Saturday evening; in fact, everybody seemed to be tumbling to the place in order to help. He had been criticised to some extent because there had been no public appeal. The catastrophe was a result of the war, and the Government were prepared to back the bill, and out of the private contributions the Emergency Committee could give urgently needed relief. The Mayor went on to speak of those people who had sought refuge in the houses of friends, and said a most distressing case of this kind was where a young married woman with a sick husband, living in two rooms, took in 6 other people, and they had remained there until Tuesday. In such cases they were prepared to remunerate the people who had harboured the homeless (Hear, Hear).

Alderman Davis said he wanted to move that the best thanks of the Council be given to the Emergency Committee for the way in which they had done their work (Hear, hear). He lived in the district, and he did not know what they would have done but for the Committee. Some of the children had been put to bed on Friday night before the explosion took place, and how they escaped he really did not know. Many of the women had their husbands in the Army or Navy at the time, and the bravery of these women was beyond description. He was in one of the roads not far from the scene of the accident during most of the night, and he hoped that he would never again see what he saw that night. He desired to include in the vote of thanks all who had in any way assisted in the work of helping those poor people.

In seconding, Alderman Moore-Smith said he was glad that Alderman Davis had included in the motion all who had assisted in any way. On Sunday morning he was called to the district, and found that Lady Muriel Paget and some friends had come down from the West End with two vehicles full of children's clothing. He took her to the proper place, and she at once set to work to distribute the clothing and dress the children. At dinner time a tradesman in the district came with the offer of provisions, and the Boy Scouts at once went and obtained a large supply from this source.

Later in the day Lady Paget came to another part of the district and got in touch with Mr. Boardman and Mr. Leavey and before night two cart-loads of clothing were sent into the devastated district. As to future work, the suggestions which had been made should be referred to the new Committee.

Councillor Hollins said as a member of the Emergency Committee, and one who had participated in the hospitality shown by the Committee, he desired to testify to the splendid work which had been done. He was pleased to say, hundreds of people in the locality had expressed their deep sense of gratitude, at the way in which their wants had been attended to. He did not think it was possible to describe what took place in the immediate neighbourhood of the explosion on Friday evening. What was then seen beggared description. The people were called upon to make an exodus from the district because it was feared that further explosions might take place, and it was difficult to know what would have happened to them had they not had these places of refuge to which they could go. He hoped the new Committee would get to work at once, and one of the most pressing problems to be dealt with was that of getting away the furniture which still remained in some of the houses.

Alderman Davis suggested that one of the public buildings should be used for the storage of furniture. He understood that some of the people would not leave the neighbourhood because of their furniture.

The Mayor: 'That is one of the matters which will come before the Committee.'

Alderman White added his testimony to the good work of the Committee, and the motion was put and carried unanimously.

Alderman Enos Smith said it had been suggested that the new school should be used for the storage of furniture, but it would be shortly opened for educational purposes. However, he thought they could let one of the other schools for this purpose.

Councillor Jones said that, although they were appointing a committee to act in conjunction with the Emergency Committee, he thought there was another matter in which they should make public declaration. Already there was machinery being put in operation for transferring people to other districts but the Emergency Committee had set their faces against such a thing (Hear, hear).

Alderman Bishop: 'That is a matter for the committee.'

A letter was read from Lord Rhondda, the President of the Local Government Board, stating that his department had been asked by the Prime Minister and the Minister of Munitions to undertake, in conjunction with the local authority, to render temporary assistance and supervise the application of any funds available for that purpose. He suggested that the Town Council should appoint a committee of their own members, to which should be added the representatives of other interests concerned. All local measures of assistance should be in the hands of the special committee, and the Board forwarded a special grant of £500 from the National Relief Fund for the purpose of meeting immediate expenses. The department were making inquiries as to the provision of suitable accommodation for those persons who had been provided with temporary accommodation. The Town Council could rely on the assistance of the Local Government Board in any steps they might make.

The Mayor then moved that the Council, as requested, form a special committee, consisting of the Mayor, Alderman Crow, White and Davis, Councillors Filmer, Flaxman, Holland, Wordley, Croot, Jones, Godbold, and Hollins. The Mayor's motion was carried.

A further letter was received from the Local Government Board stating that in addition to the generous donations already received, the National Relief Fund was available for the purpose of relieving the immediate distress. In the opinion of Lord Rhondda it was unnecessary to open any new fund. This letter was referred to the Committee.

The Mayor said that in forming this committee it was the unanimous opinion of the Council that the committee and the emergency committee should work hand in hand. He sincerely hoped that the two committees would work together without friction. The superintendents of the various halls where the people were staying were responsible for feeding the people under their care. When the matter was settled they would present their bills, and the money would be paid.

The Town Clerk read a further letter from the Local Government Board with regard to the provision of accommodation for those who had been displaced by the disaster. The Board made certain suggestions with regard to housing some of the people on the other side of the river.

The Town Clerk added that during the day he had received a further communication from the Local Government Board stating that the Port of London Authority had 47 vacant houses in the borough, and there would be little difficulty in obtaining these houses for the purpose.

Councillor Jones said he wished to oppose the suggestion of forcing these people out of the district. The committee felt that if they put their shoulders to the wheel they could find the necessary accommodation in the borough. The suggestion that they should take the 47 houses belonging to the Port of London Authority was as good one as they could get, and he thought they should accept it. He would formally move a resolution waiving certain rights so that they use these houses. The motion was carried without discussion.

Councillor Jones added that he understood that certain property owners were prepared to meet the committee with the idea of helping them in the matter, and if they could be of assistance the committee should meet them (Hear, hear).

1 *Above:* The Brunner Mond factory at Crescent Wharf, photographed in 1895. Up to 1912 it was used for the manufacture of caustic soda and had then lain idle until 1915 when it was modified to purify TNT.

2 *Right:* Dr Andrea Angel was an Oxford don who had volunteered for war work and was employed by Brunner Mond as chief chemist at the Silvertown factory. He died in the explosion.

5   North Woolwich Road, south of Victoria Dock, shortly after the explosion.

3   *Opposite above:* Silvertown fire station before the explosion.
4   *Opposite below:* Silvertown fire station and one of the fire engines.

6   Demolished houses in Fort Road.

GALLANT FIREMEN KILLED AND INJURED IN THE GREAT EXPLOSION.

Fireman Sell, killed.

Fireman Sell's little daughter was also killed.

Station Officer S. S. Betts (standing), injured, and Fireman Yabsley, seriously injured.

Sub-officer Vickers, dead

Fireman Chapple, injured.

Fireman J. J. Betts, injured

7   *Above:* Silvertown firemen killed and injured in the explosion, from a feature in the *Stratford Express.*

8   *Right:* Letter from West Ham Council to the injured fireman T.R. Betts.

WS/M.

TOWN HALL.
WEST HAM E.

13th February, 1917.

Dear Sir,

I beg to inform you that at the last meeting of the Council references were made by the Mayor and other members to the disastrous Explosion at Silvertown, and they unanimously adopted a resolution expressing their sincere sympathy with you and the other members of the Fire Brigade and their families who had received injuries through the disaster, and in doing so they gave expression to their sense of the bravery displayed by you and the other members of the Brigade in facing the risk of death on that occasion. The Council earnestly hope that you may have a speedy and complete recovery.

I am, Dear Sir,
Yours faithfully,

George E. Hilleary

Town Clerk.

Fireman T.R. Betts.

9, 10   The ruins of Silvertown fire station after the explosion. Temporary huts have been erected on the site.

11, 12   Silvertown fire station was used as a temporary store for timber panels for making sheds and temporary cover.

13 A closer view of the gutted fire station.

14 Damaged grain silos on the pontoon dock, North Woolwich.

THE EXPLOSION.

Persons in distress by reason of the Explosion may apply for assistance at the PUBLIC HALL, CANNING TOWN, after 2 o'clock TO-DAY (FRIDAY. 26th JANUARY), and thereafter daily from 10.30 a.m. to 1.0 p.m. and 2.0 p.m. to 4.0 p.m., until further notice.

No applications for compensation for Damage to Property or Personal Effects can be entertained at this Office. Such Claims must be made to the Ministry of Munitions, at the PUBLIC LIBRARY. NORTH STREET, PLAISTOW.

R. MANSFIELD,
Mayor.

15   Poster advertising the relief arrangements.

16 The badly damaged St Barnabas' Church fenced off from the street for security.

17 The interior of St Barnabas' parish hall where between sixty and seventy Band of Hope children were having their treat when the factory exploded. Amazingly, none were killed or seriously injured.

ADVENTURE
Children left homeless by Silvertown munition factory explosion.

18   One of the many emergency relief centres set up to provide shelter for the homeless.

19   Barking Road Wesleyan Methodist Church provided food for the homeless after the explosion.

20 *Left:* Damaged houses in Fort Street.

21 *Below:* The wrecked interior of a fireman's house in Fort Street. 'In many cases the roofs and the bedrooms had just disappeared. Only parts of the walls of the downstairs rooms were left. These rooms were no longer rooms. They had no ceilings; their fronts had vanished' (Fireman J.J. Betts).

22 *Right:* A member of the Essex Volunteer Regiment on duty outside one of the firemen's houses in Fort Street. There were several reports of looting from damaged houses.

23 *Below:* Rear view of the terrace of firemen's houses.

24 A policeman on duty outside houses in Fort Street, some of which have been partly boarded up.

25 The remains of Silvertown Lubricants, Minoco Wharf, the neighbouring plot to the Brunner Mond works. 'Around me was a vast plain of rubble' (Fireman J.J. Betts).

26 A view of the docks from Silvertown Way in the early 1930s.

27 A view looking south from North Woolwich in the 1970s. (Reproduced by kind permission of Eastside)

28   *Above:* Another view of North Woolwich in the 1970s. (Reproduced by kind permission of Eastside)

29   *Left:* Crescent Wharf as it looks today. (Reproduced by kind permission of TDG UK Storage and Distribution)

The Gallant Firemen

When the report of the Works Committee came up for consideration Alderman Moore-Smith said he was glad to be able to state
that satisfactory arrangements had been made with the L.C.C. to
get over any difficulties that might occur in regard to future fires in
the district.

Councillor Jones thought a more detailed report should be
given as to the conduct of the firemen on this occasion. Some men
had been awarded the Victoria Cross for less than these men had
done (Hear, hear).

The Mayor said he desired to move a sincere vote of sympathy
with the relatives of the two firemen who had been killed, and also
with those who had been injured.

Anybody who was down in the district on the night of the
explosion and saw the position in which the men were placed
could not other than be surprised that they were not all blown to
pieces. These men had to carry out dangerous and laborious work,
and they had done it without thought of their own lives.

Councillor Billing said he desired to second the resolution. One
of the most outstanding features of this terrible calamity had been
bravely manifested by the firemen. Within a few minutes they were
on the scene of the fire, and it was in the course of their duties that
two of them had lost their lives. They had many instances brought
to their notice of the bravery of their firemen but this incident
would for ever stand out in their memories. As Councillor Jones
had said if ever men deserved the V.C. then surely it was these men.
As a council they extend their heartfelt sympathy to the relatives of
the deceased firemen.

Councillor Gardner said as an ex-chairman of the Works
Committee he desired to support the resolution. The report which
the acting superintendent had given to the Works Committee was
quite pathetic. He said that after he had arrived and his men got
their engine to work, he went round to the place where the local
fire engine had begun to get ready. Apparently they had not time to

actually start work, and he found the firemen lying by the engine. Two of them were dead. They died doing their duty (Hear, hear).

Councillor Jones said it seemed to him that West Ham was always in the background, except when there was a terrible disaster. They ought to ask the Mayor, when replying to the letter of sympathy from His Majesty, to recommend the firemen to the consideration of the proper authorities for suitable recognition. Dr. Angell, the firemen and others risked their lives, and they should bring the actions of such men to the notice of the proper authorities. The motion was carried.

The Town Clerk also announced that a letter had been received from the Minister of Munitions stating that they had opened an office at the North Street Library for the consideration of any claims that might be put in. The Minister desired to thank the Corporation, particularly the Mayor, for the assistance given in this respect. Some members wanted to know why the library had been chosen for this purpose; and the Mayor explained that the representatives of the Ministry of Munitions were given the choice of several places. They were not trying to evade their responsibility, and such being the case it was the duty of the Corporation to help them.

The Education Difficulty
Nineteen schools closed for repairs

On Wednesday evening a special meeting of the local education committee was held for the purpose of dealing with educational matters arising out of the explosion. The chair was taken by Alderman Enos Smith (Chairman), and there were present: Misses Cheetham and Duncan, Aldermen Crow and Hurry, Councillors Bell, Hughes, Gardner, Filmer, and Roof, the Revs. A.J. Palmer, E. Lees, and Father Hickey, and Mr. N.M. Hyde.

In opening the meeting the Chairman said they met under the shadow of a very great calamity – a calamity so great that nothing like it had happened in our country for many years. He felt sure that he would be meeting the wishes of the committee if on their behalf he expressed their very great sorrow at the loss of life, their heartfelt sympathy with the bereaved, their sincere hope that those who had been injured would have a speedy recovery, and their intense admiration for the heroic self sacrifice of those who gave their services in the performance of their duties, and in some cases gave their lives. At the same time, sad as had been the calamity he thought there should be a note of thankfulness that the accident was at the time when the schools were not in session. He was absolutely sure from his own observation that had they been open at the time several hundred of the children would have been killed and many more injured. When he mentioned that in some cases large casements had blown in and lodged across the desks where the children would have been sitting they would understand that the loss of life would have been terrible. Again, they had to be thankful for the fact that at that particular time the factories did not have their full complement of work people.

The vote of sympathy was carried; and the Chairman went on to say that he had prepared a report of what he had done, because he thought it was only right that the Committee should know the state of affairs, and he would like to know that he had their sympathy and support in the work he had carried out.

The Chairman commenced his report by stating that many of the schools in the southern part of the borough were seriously damaged and, accompanied by the Council's Inspector (Mr. Madden), he spent Saturday and Sunday in visiting the schools and inspecting the damage done. Mr. Jacques reported that he had made a preliminary survey of the schools lying within the area affected by the explosion. One school was so badly damaged in all departments, including the caretaker's house, that its restoration would take probably four to six months. He was making a detailed survey and estimate of the damage done to the buildings, furniture and stock, with a view to restoration being undertaken at the earliest possible date and for the claim on the insurance company. Another school was being used as a mortuary, and he deferred his survey for the present. At six schools the structural damage mainly consisted of fallen ceilings, broken sashes and frames, and frames blown out of the openings, with some consequent damage to brickwork and an extensive breakage of glass, and some damage to furniture and stock. He had placed orders for boarding doors, window and roof openings, to protect the premises from the weather and from thieves, pending the issue of detailed specifications for the structural repairs. He was preparing detailed estimates for claims on the insurance company. In these cases also the restoration would take some time – probably as regard to the worst cases, several weeks to render the premises fit for school use.

In twenty-four other schools the damage was mainly limited to broken glass and a few broken sashes and doors, and, provided labour and glass could be obtained, the restoration should occupy but a few days for this job. He ascertained through the Borough Treasurer that the insurance company consented to the necessary work of this kind being deal with, leaving the question of the company's liability to be decided at a later date, and he had therefore given orders for the re-instatement of glass to be put in hand forthwith, and where that was not possible to put temporary protection to the openings. They should not, however, be used – or, at least, those rooms with broken windows – until the shattered glass was removed, as there was considerable danger of its falling and injuring the children.

At several of the schools he was able to get men at work early on Saturday, and the work had been continued over the week-end, but owing to the heavy demand for men and materials, particularly glass, the supply was limited. At the remainder of the schools the damage was either not evident or limited to a few panes of glass, and would be dealt with as ordinary school repairs. These schools need not be closed. It would be noted that three of the schools where considerable damage had been done were non-provided schools and, pending instructions, he was not at present taking steps for their repair.

The Chairman added that in consequence of this report and his own observations, he gave direction for 19 schools and special sub-

ject centres attached thereto, to be closed until further notice.
Owing to the necessity of better arrangements being made for the
accommodation of homeless families, temporarily provided for in
the halls of institutes and churches, he arranged for one school to
be closed on Tuesday at the close of the afternoon session, and the
whole of the conveniences of the dining centre to be placed at the
disposal of the Emergency Committee. A large number of families
were placed there the same evening. In consultation with the
Council's Inspectors, he arranged for the children displaced to take
part-time instruction at one school. He received a letter from
Father Fitzgerald stating that a number of homeless children were
being temporarily housed in the Roman Catholic school, and asking for permission to close the school for one week, to which he
assented. Having regard for the number of children displaced, he
thought it well to give directions for arrangements to be made for
the early opening of the new school as a temporary expedient only,
and the Architect was now engaged in arranging for the delivery of
the furniture. He had also given instructions that no child was to be
refused admission to any of the schools which remain open, and
His Majesty's Inspector, Mr. A.M. Moore, had expressed the wish of
the Board of Education to assist them in every possible way to
carry on the work under such difficult circumstances. At his
request the staff of the schools closed attended at the office on
Monday, when he explained to them the difficulties of the position, and asked them to place themselves entirely at the disposal of
the Council's Inspectors to render assistance in any schools where
their services might be required. At the same time, feeling hardship
might be placed on the 'Supply' teachers by having been deprived
of their employment, he gave an undertaking, on behalf of the
Committee, that their salaries would be continued during the time
they were thrown out of employment owing to the closing of the
schools.

The Chairman added that the new arrangements had been carried out that day at two schools, and it worked admirably. He had
asked Mr. Jacques if he could give any opinion as to when the

schools could be opened, and he hoped that two would be open by Monday, and the bulk of the others would be open a week later.

Two of the schools would take some months to repair. It was somewhat peculiar that in several cases it was the lower floors which suffered the most. He could assure the Committee that he had done very little else since the explosion except to attend to that business, and it had given him great anxiety.

Alderman Hurry moved that the Chairman's report be adopted. Mr. Hyde seconded, and referred to the point that no scholar was to be refused admission at any school. Did that mean that they could crowd the schools as much as they chose?

The Chairman replied in the affirmative. He stated that the Inspector said that even if they could not give the ordinary lessons they should get as many children as possible to school (Hear, Hear). He had given the visiting officers instructions to send the children to school, and the head teachers had received instructions to admit them.

The Reverend A.J. Palmer supported the adoption of the report, and said he thought the Committee should express their sincere gratitude to the Chairman for the admirable way in which he had met the exigencies of the occasion. The Chairman had done his duty, and they thoroughly admired the spirit he had shown, and thanked him for the time and energy and sacrifice he had made at this time.

The Chairman: 'It is very kind of Mr. Palmer to say that, but I hope he will overlook the fact that when I say it was the first time I have spent a Sunday dashing about in a taxicab.' (Laughter)

Mr. Palmer: 'Complete absolution, Mr. Chairman.' (Laughter)

SATURDAY 3 FEBRUARY 1917

Editorial Column

Seldom have such scenes been witnessed in the streets of the borough as those which characterised the passing to their graves of
some of the victims of the recent explosion. Those who witnessed
the procession which accompanied the gallant firemen to their
resting places could not fail to have been impressed by the public
testimony to their bravery. No greater honours could possibly have
been conferred upon any men, but certainly their gallant conduct
deserved this last public testimony. Practically every department of
public life in the borough was represented in the procession, and
the service at the Parish Church was one of the most impressive
ever held within the walls of that venerable structure. The idea has
already been mooted, and we trust will be brought to a satisfactory
conclusion, that the suitable recognition of the firemen's heroism
should be accorded by those in authority. These honours can only
be posthumous in the case of two of the firemen, but their children
should treasure them all the more by reason of that fact, and in the
case of the men who have survived the terrible ordeal they would
have the satisfaction of knowing that their heroism in the face of
almost certain death had been fully appreciated. Again on
Wednesday many thousands of people thronged the streets to
express their sympathy with the private victims of the disaster. The
public funeral given that day was certainly an indication, as empha-
sised by the Bishop of Chelmsford, of the way in which the great
calamity had brought men of all religions into a common fellow-
ship. Bishops and non-conformist ministers were there side by side
in their endeavours to console those who had been bereaved by
this awful calamity.

The Great Explosion

Gallant Fireman's Funeral – Imposing Procession through the Borough
Address by the Bishop of Chelmsford

On Tuesday afternoon the victims of the recent explosion in a munition factory in the East End were laid to rest in the Corporation cemetery [West Ham Cemetery, Cemetery Road, Forest Gate].

The victims were all associated with the local fire brigade, and two of them, Sub officer Vicars and fireman Sell, were the gallant firemen who met their deaths when, with their colleagues, they were making arrangements to cope with the fire which produced the awful explosion. At the same time there were buried Winifred Sell, the daughter of fireman Sell, and the infant child of fireman Betts.

The funeral of these gallant firemen was accompanied by every public honour that could be conferred upon them.

The Mayor and Corporation were present, and walked in the funeral procession, together with several hundred firemen from all parts of London and the suburbs, Special Constables, Volunteers, and turncocks.

The bodies of the two firemen were enclosed in elm coffins, with the usual fittings. The coffins, draped with union jacks and covered with a profusion of beautiful floral tributes, were borne to the cemetery on motor fire engines. Alongside the motor engines walked members of the same brigade headed by Acting-Supt. Robinson. The procession was headed by the band of the 'K' Division of the Metropolitan Police, and practically every department of public life in the Borough was represented in the long procession which followed the coffins. The day was bitterly cold, and the snow was falling during the greater part of the journey to the Parish Church, but in spite of these climatic conditions thousands of people lined the route, and reverently paid their last respects to the gallant dead. No more imposing funeral procession has ever wended its way through the streets of the Borough; no greater honours have ever been paid to any local men.

The procession met at the fire station in the southern part of the Borough. The band played the Dead March as the procession commenced its long journey. Immediately behind the band came the two fire engines bearing the bodies of the two firemen, and then a private hearse containing the coffins of the girl and the little child. The mourning coaches containing the relatives of the deceased came next and then the Mayor and Corporation, firemen, Volunteers, and Special Constables.

The Mayor (Alderman Mansfield) was present in his robes of office and, accompanied by a large number of members and officials of the Corporation, walked the whole of the distance from the fire station in the south to the cemetery in the northern part of the borough where the bodies were interred. The Mayor was supported by the Deputy Mayor (Councillor J.T. Husband) and the Town Clerk (Mr. G.E. Hilleary), and accompanied by Aldermen W. Thorne, M.P., W. Crow, J.P., D.J. Davis, J.P., W. Devenay, J.R. Hurry, Enos Smith, and R. White, J.P.; Councillors J. Holland, T. McCallum, Herbert Dyer, F. Gray, E.W. Wordley, G.H. Fennell, W. Ping, M. Streimer, E.S.J. Flaxman, A. Bothwell, S. Bulling, W. Godbold, W. Sanders, J.H. Rooff, A.J. Hart, J.J. Jones, T. Kirk, B.W. Gardner, E.J. Reed, J.G. Filmer, and J.H. Hollins; the Borough Treasurer (Mr. C.H. Patterson), the Borough Engineer (Mr. J.G. Morley), the Medical Officer of Health (Dr. C. Sanders), the Electrical Engineer (Mr. J.W. Beauchamp), the Tramways Manager (Mr. M.L. Slattery) and the Principal of the Technical Institute (Mr. J.R. Airy). There were also present: the Revs. E. Lees and A. J. Palmer, Mr. W. Calderwood, and Mr. Norman Hyde (members of the Education Committee), the Rev. R. Rowntree Clifford, and ex-councillor Leggatt.

Superintendent Gear (of Beckenham), Superintendent Gravenor (of Ealing), and Superintendent Johnson (of Gloucester), all of whom were formerly members of the local fire brigade, also took part in the procession.

One of the victims, Winifred Sell, was a scholarship holder at the Central Secondary School, and a number of her young friends were present at the church, and afterwards took part in the procession. They were accompanied by Dr. Burness (Principal) and Miss Jeremy (the mistress of the form in which the young girl was a pupil).

Several hundred firemen took part in the procession, the fire brigades represented being the local fire brigade, the Metropolitan Fire Brigade, East Ham, Southall, Barnett, Erith, Willesden, Metropolitan Water Board, Brighton, Rugby, Ealing, Twickenham, Epping, Kodaks, Houston and Isleworth, Croydon, Clarnico, Ilford, Wanstead, Chingford, Wembley, Leyton, Penge, Beckenham, Chiswick, Hendon, New Barnet, Bromley, Frien Barnet, Barking, Walthamstow, Bexhill, Reigate and Finchley. The London Salvage Corps were represented by their chief, Col. Fox; and the Croydon brigade were represented by Councillor Addison, the chairman of the Fire Brigade Committee of that county borough.

On reaching the Parish Church [All Saints' Church, Church Street, West Ham] the funeral cortege was met by the surpliced clergy and choir. Those taking part in the church were the Bishop of Chelmsford, the Bishop of Barking, Canon P.M. Bayne, the Rev. Travers Guy Rogers (Vicar of the Borough), the Rev. W.G. Farley, and the Rev. R.E.T. Bell.

The service in the church opened with the singing of the psalm, 'God is our hope and strength,' and the lesson was then read by the Bishop of Barking. Following the hymn 'Brief life is here our portion,' an address was given by the Bishop of Chelmsford.

The Bishop said there could scarcely be a more solemn service than that in which they were taking part, words that extraordinarily came to one's lips rose slowly on such an occasion. There were feelings in their hearts too deep for words, but at the same time he thought that on such an occasion some few words should be uttered. One of the paradoxes of the war was that whilst on the one hand they were thinking of it in the sense of taking human life, on the other hand there never was a time in the history of their lives when the importance and value of human life was so fully recognised, as at the present time. The reason was that they believed they were in the war for things not material, but for those great spiritual realities of truth, liberty and righteousness, without which the world would not be worth living in. They were becoming more and more accustomed to the idea that these things, and not wealth, were the things really worth living for, and so they were willing to spend their wealth, and even risk their lives in order that these principles might shine forth. The whole nation was realising today that human life was the most vital thing in the national career, and that was aptly illustrated in the case of the firemen. When he went to a fire the first thing he did was to ascertain if there were any people in the burning house, and if such were the case he would concentrate his whole energies upon saving human life before attempting to save the property. Was not that principle being extended in their national life in every department, so that they were recognising through all grades of society that

HUMAN LIFE CAME FIRST,

and property second? That day they were mourning the loss of two of their brothers. He had often thought that there should be some decoration given to firemen equal in importance, equal in value, to that of the Victoria Cross. He knew quite well that their brothers on the battlefield did heroic deeds, he knew that the Victoria Cross meant much, but he thought that the men who risked their lives to save life should have recognition equal in value to those of their brothers on the battlefield. That day they had gathered to pay their last tribute of respect to those who have passed away – to express their real sympathy with those who were bereaved. They thought of their two brothers who had died in the path of duty. Where they would rather have died than walking that road – the path of duty?

They laid, as it were, wreaths of respect upon the coffins of their brothers. They thought, too, of the young girl of fifteen, cut off just as she was merging into womanhood. Then, again, there was the dear little infant. Brief life had indeed been her portion. Was that not something like what was going on throughout the world today

– men in the prime of life being cut off, women, girls and little children? This terrible disaster had made many of them realise as they had never realised before what the war had meant to Belgium, France, Poland, and Serbia. Many of those present probably remembered the Biblical story of the three men cast into the fiery furnace. That day they as a community were in a fiery furnace. How many households in that borough were suffering, not merely through this explosion, but through this horrible war? But let them remember in all their troubles and perplexities that there was One with them 'like unto the Son of God.' Let them grasp this fact that this war was the greatest vindication that Christianity ever had. Europe was torn and bleeding and gasping. Why was it? For the last twenty years what had their statesmen thought about God, or righteousness, or the teaching of Jesus Christ? Had they ever read a dispatch from any Foreign Office upholding the principles of Jesus Christ? No. The diplomatists [sic] had tried to run Europe by the wisdom of man and had left God out of it, and they had made a mess off it. He urged them to realise as they had never realised before that this was not the end. What man called death was really birth – being ushered into a more beautiful and better life. Their brothers had died in the path of duty, and he called upon each one of them to live in the path of duty, so that when the end came they would enter into the presence of the King knowing they had done their duty.

Following the address, special prayers were offered by the Vicar; and the service concluded with the Dead March. As the four coffins were being carried down the aisle to the west end of the church the organist played 'O, rest in the Lord.'

The procession was then re-formed, and the two Bishops and the clergy walked in their vestments to the cemetery. Here three special graves had been arranged by the Corporation. Sub Officer Vicars was buried in one, Fireman Sell and his daughter in another, and the infant in the third. The committal sentences were read by the Bishop of Chelmsford, and the service concluded with the Blessing.

The Rev. F. Pollard (of St. James) and the Rev. V. Smith (Cemetery Chaplain) were also present at the graveside.

The three graves are family graves provided by the Corporation, and are next to the grave of Supt. Smith, who was interred a few weeks ago.

A large number of beautiful wreaths were sent. In addition to those from the relatives and friends of the deceased, floral emblems were received from the Corporation of the Borough, The Borough Fire Brigade, Alderman Hoskin (Chairman of Works Committee), the staff of Plaistow Hospital, the Metropolitan Water Board, the Highways Department (Crawford Street), Tottenham Fire Brigade, the Insurance Committee, the uniform staff of the Libraries, London Fire Brigade, Supt. Boxhall and officers and men of the local Sub-Division of Police, night shed department Corporation Tramways, Ilford Fire Brigade, local tradesmen (two), London Salvage Corps, the local tramways staff, National Workers Union, Woolwich Division of Police, the pumping station staff, the Central Secondary School, the National Fire Brigade Union, Willesden Fire Brigade, Port of London Authority, and Mr. Morley.

The funeral arrangements for Sub officer Vickars were made by Mr. Hiscock; and Messrs. Burry made the necessary arrangements in the other three cases.

Eleven other Victims Interred
A Bishop's impressions of the Explosion
The King's Representative attends

On Wednesday afternoon eleven other victims were laid to rest, seven at East London Cemetery and four at West Ham. Despite the wintry weather, the route was lined with spectators, and hundreds of women many of them accompanied by young children, assembled at the burial ground.

A service was held at the Public Hall. Thousands of people assembled outside, but admission was confined to ticket holders. Even so, the large hall was filled, public men and private individuals representative of almost every section of the community being present. His Majesty the King was represented by the Hon. Henry Stoner. The Mayor, in his robes of office, the Town Clerk, and many members of the Corporation, attended, whilst clergy of many denominations also took part in the service. In front of the platform hung a beautiful wreath of lilies, sent by the Emergency Committee. It bore the words: 'Peace, perfect peace. With deepest sympathy'. Mr. G. Bernard Gilbert, F.R.C.O., presided at the organ, and rendered appropriate music; and the presiding minister was the Rev. R. Rowntree Clifford. The opening hymn, 'Our God, our help in ages past,' was sympathetically sung, and prayer was offered by the Bishop of Barking. Passages of scripture were read by the Rev. W. G. Farley and Mr. Norman M. Hyde. The hymn 'Lead, kindly light,' was then sung, and the Bishop of Chelmsford delivered an address. His Lordship expressed an appreciation of the deep sympathy shown by his Majesty in asking the Hon. Henry Stoner to attend the service on his behalf, and said that in so doing his Majesty had shown his sympathy to the whole nation, as had always been the case in the past. Continuing, the Bishop said he had an opportunity of speaking in another place, but he desired to say how deeply he was touched last week in going through the streets affected by the explosion. Two things attracted his notice particularly.

The first was the magnificent way in which the emergency had been dealt with. It hardly seemed possible that within a few hours of the occurrence such excellent arrangements could have been made by the Mayor and Corporation, assisted right loyally by citizens of good will. He saw members of all creeds and parties helping in the work, and he thought how wonderfully this had brought out those things of their common Christianity and made them all as one. Then he thought of the wonderful bravery with which people were bearing this disaster. Men, women and children had been cast out of their homes, but were bearing it all so bravely, and he would like to testify to the full what he felt in his own heart of their bravery. This explosion could in no way be said to have come from God or by the will of God. Surely it was the product of man. It was due to the wrong-mindedness and selfishness of man.

When they came to think upon such an occurrence, it made them all the more determined to carry on the war to such an end that God willing, it should be the end of all wars.

They were fighting that fighting might cease. He wanted them to realise that there were far worse things than death. Many of them got into the habit of thinking that death was the most awful thing in the world, but it depended on how they looked at it. If they looked upon it as the end of all things, very good; but if they realised that it was only the beginning of something, then they got a different aspect. To the bereaved he would say 'do not sorrow as men without hope.' Here, in this life, they were bound by the limitations of mind, by business cares, and a hundred other things. They could not do as they would. Then came death, and they were free from their bodies, and could grow and thrive. They had this view of life going on and on. But they should make the best of the present life. They must see to it that their environment was right, that their social conditions were right, and that the slums were swept away. The state must see to it that men, through their environment, had a chance to grow and develop. They must realise that Christ must be the centre of life here, as life there. There must be eliminations from the national life, which could come by no other means than through Jesus Christ. He had seen life in all stages, but had never seen a man whom Christ would not, or could not, help. They had had a great call in that borough. 'In the midst of life we are in death'. No one who had lived within the sound of the explosion would ever forget it; God was looking to them now to set their house in order. They might rebuild the damaged district, but he prayed that every new house might be filled with the spirit and glory of the Lord.

'Abide with me, fast falls the eventide,' was feelingly sung, and the service concluded with the Benediction. As the mourners and followers left the building the Dead March was impressively rendered by the organist.

The coffins were not taken into the hall. Each was conveyed in a separate hearse followed by its own mourners. When the cortege left the hall snow was falling heavily, but there were more people than ever waiting to see it pass. Led by the Salvational Army International Staff Band, conducted by Deputy Bandmaster Fuller, it proceeded along Barking Road, through Balaam Street, and the four coffins destined for West Ham Cemetery there left the main procession. At East London Cemetery there was a big crowd, principally composed of women and children. The graves were dug side by side in a long row, but only four of them were utilised for the seven coffins. A mother and her son and daughter were placed in one of them; two friends in another; and each of the others was interred separately.

A space was roped off to prevent the intrusion of the crowd, and a platform erected at the head of the graves for the accommodation of the clergy. The Salvation Band led the singing, and the Rev. W.G. Farley was the presiding clergyman. 'A few more years shall roll' and 'For ever with the Lord' were sung; and, after a scriptural passage had been read by the Revd. J. Bastow Wilson, the commitment sentences were pronounced by the Bishop of Chelmsford.

The scene was extremely impressive and weird, and made a fitting termination to the terrible tragedy. In the fast gathering darkness the mourners stood around the open graves listening to the last prayer for their loved ones. The silence, except for the minister's voice was broken only by the occasional shrill neighing of a horse; and the mantle of snow covering the cemetery accentuated the pallor of the mourners' faces.

In the background were the banners of the various trade union organisations tossed by the biting wind. The touch of death's hand seemed to lie upon the whole assembly.

Finally the Lord's Prayer was repeated, the Bishop gave the Benediction, and the service was at an end. The mourners made their way back to the coaches, the lights of which could be seen glinting through the trees.

The seven bodies interred in East London Cemetery were those of Mrs. Mary Wass, aged 32; and her son Stanley and daughter Elsie, aged 10 and 13 respectively; Alexander Hart, 25; Edward Godsmark, 15; James Bruce, 62, and Norman Gardener, aged 5. Those interred at West Ham Cemetery were those of four children of one family named Patrick – William, aged 9; Ruby, 6; Rosa, 4; and Roydon, 2.

The procession, which was marshalled by Alderman J.R. Hurry, was as follows: the Salvation Army International Staff Band, the Cross Bearer, clergy and ministers; funeral cortege, the Mayor and Corporation, Emergency Committee, representatives of public bodies; doctors, nurses and sisters; Salvation Army sisters, trades union and friendly societies, military and the public.

Other victims interred in the East London Cemetery since the explosion, excluding Dr. Angel, and those mentioned above, were: Charlotte Hiscock, Charles Hiscock, Walter Sharp, Eleanor Noakes, Sophia Villers, Thomas Tasker, George Wainwright, John Howard, Eliza Lettson, Lily Davey, Fredk. Craft, Edward Craft, Hugh McCoombs, Walter Mauger, Sidney Benstead, Thomas Acton, Albert Tyzack, William Sinden, May Jennings, Agnes Jennings, William Lambert, George Wemborne, Frederick Robinson, and Edward Forshaw.

David Earl Taylor, aged 69, another victim, was also buried at West Ham Cemetery on Wednesday; and Hugh McMarsh, aged 24, on Thursday.

Funeral of Dr. Angel

Recovered from the crater formed by the great explosion, the body of Dr. Andrea Angel was interred in East London Cemetery on Saturday morning. The service was of the simplest nature possible, and except for the fact that the grave was lined with purple cloth there was nothing to distinguish it from the ordinary funerals that take place there every day. The utmost secrecy was maintained, and none of the public was aware that the hero was to be taken to his last resting place that day. Following the recovery of the body, and formal evidence of identification before the Coroner, it was conveyed to a social institute in the neighbourhood, where it rested until Saturday. The cortege consisted of an open hearse and one carriage, and it was met at the cemetery gates by the Mayor of the borough and a representative of the Town Clerk's Department, together with directors of the factory. The coffin was borne into the little church, and the service was conducted by the Rev. Father Lawrence, who also pronounced the commitment sentences. There were less than a dozen people in all at the graveside, amongst them being the widow. The grave is situated immediately in front of a batch of others prepared for the reception of other victims of the catastrophe, some of whom have already been interred.

The floral tributes included a wreath of pink and red carnations, with a backing of palms. It bore the inscription 'From his wife.' A wreath of laurels, tied with scarlet ribbon, was inscribed with 'The Borough's respectful homage'.

There were also tributes form the directors of the factory and its employees, one of single daffodils 'from his children,' and a wreath from his 'sorrowing parents and sisters'.

The breast plate of the coffin bore only the words 'Andrea Angel.'

A Spiritualist's Funeral

Two of the victims, Mr. E. Croft and his baby boy, were interred on Friday according to the Spiritualist rights in an East London cemetery. The interment ceremony was conducted by Mr. G. Taylor Gwinn, president of the Union of London Spiritualists, and the London Lyceum District Council, of which Mr. Croft was a prominent worker, was represented by the president, Mr. J. Forsyth (North London), the Secretary, Mr. A. T. Connor (Fulham), and representatives of the various London Lyceums. The Woolwich and Plumstead Lyceum, to which Mr. Croft belonged, have lost a distinguished member and an ardent worker in the cause of the children.

More Victims Identified

On Monday afternoon the Coroner's jury was again summoned for the purpose of hearing evidence of identification of persons killed in the great explosion. The Coroner expressed their sympathy with relatives of the deceased.

The first case was that of James Kidd, 49, a grain porter, who was identified by his widow. Henry George Skinner, a ganger in the grain department, said he sent deceased to the office to draw money for the men at work. He saw the fire start, and soon after heard the explosion. He went to search for Kidd, but came back because of the danger. Stephen Arthur Barton, an engine driver, deposed to finding Kidd on the line suffering from an injury to the left leg. He tied up the leg with his handkerchief and carried the deceased to the Port police station. Dock P.C. Huggett said he took the man to a hospital, where first aid was rendered. As the hospital was full, he then took the deceased to another institution.

David Taylor, 69, a watchman employed at the munition factory where the fire occurred, was identified by his son, a chauffeur. Another watchman, named Simpson, 50, engaged by the same firm, was identified by his son, a clerk in the same Company's service.

Leonard Patrick, baker engaged at a flour mills, said that when he got home he found his house in ruins. On January 22nd he saw the body of his son, Roydon Stanley Patrick, 1 year and 11 months, in a hospital.

The body of Walter Ernest Sharp, 36, a machinist, was identified by his brother-in-law.

Ernest Parks, gas worker, East Greenwich, identified portions of the leg, foot and hand of his brother-in-law, Edgar Oliver Wenborn, 49, factory foreman. He identified the foot by the boots and sock, and from the fact that a piece of a Providential almanac had been put in the boot to ease it.

Miss Clara Flora Gardener said that when she got to her house on the evening of the explosion she found the house in ruins. On January 24th she identified the body of her brother, Norman Wilfred Gardener, aged 5, at the hospital.

Fireman Geo. Betts identified the body of his four month old daughter, Ethel Elmer Betts, whom he saw in a mortuary. His wife said that she had put the children to bed at 6 p.m. After the explosion she took the two children into the street. Someone rushed in to fetch out the deceased, but she was missed.

John Bruce, a clerk, of North Woolwich, identified by a watch and a portion of the clothing certain remains as being those of his father, James Bruce, a nightwatchman at the factory.

The Coroner said the bodies of Dr. Angel and a foreman has been identified, but the witnesses were at the government enquiry being held that day. He did not intend to go into the cause of the explosion, but the inquest would occupy the whole of next Monday.

A Brave Policeman

A verdict of death from misadventure was returned on Tuesday on two more victims of the recent explosion in the east of London.

One of them, Edward George Greenoff, aged 30, a Metropolitan Police Constable, was keeping people back from the fire and warning them that there was likely to be an explosion. When it occurred he was knocked over, and on regaining consciousness he managed to crawl some distance. He was finally removed to his home.

Cyril Roberts, who took Constable Greenoff's advice and went away, said that his own escape from death was due to the Constable's devotion to duty.

An Inspector, expressing the sympathy of the deceased's comrades, with the widow of the deceased, testified to the value of the work he had done, and said the force could ill afford to lose such men.

The Bishop's Hope:
'Safety and sanitation in re-building'

Preaching on Saturday at the institution of the Rev. Trafford Guy Rogers as Vicar of West Ham, the Bishop of Chelmsford took the opportunity of expressing his deep sympathy with the borough in the great disaster that had befallen it.

He would never forget the day that week, he said, when he went through the different streets in the devastated area. There were two things in particular that struck him. One was – and he should like to bear testimony to it – the remarkable way in which the great difficulties caused by the explosion had been grappled with by those in authority in connection with the borough. It seemed almost incredible that the arrangements were made so quickly, so thoroughly, so adequately, so kindly, and so generously. He could not help feeling as he went from one religious centre to another how it had brought all together in a wonderful way. The other thing that struck him was the remarkable calmness and quietness of the people; should he say the heroism of the women and children who had been torn so quickly and so suddenly from their homes. They were bearing their burdens, as he hoped all would endeavour their burdens to be carried also during this terrible war. He hoped and trusted, as he believed, that the borough council, with that spirit which had animated it in the past years, would give the most careful and serious consideration to the rebuilding of those streets. Whether high explosive factories should be situated in a densely populated district was for those in authority to determine, but he hoped that in the rebuilding operations everything would be done, not only for the safety of the people, but also in connection with the sanitary conditions under which they lived.

A Mayor's Thanks

Will you kindly permit me to use the columns of your paper for the purpose of expressing my most heartfelt thanks for the whole-hearted manner in which the residents of the borough and of other districts have come to the assistance of our fellow townspeople, the victims of the awful calamity on Friday evening, 19th inst?

I have been deeply touched by the self sacrifice of those who, in spite of personal injuries and damaged houses, gave shelter and comfort to their more unfortunate fellows, and by the fortitude with which those people who have been injured and rendered homeless have borne their sufferings.

A committee has been appointed by the Council at the instance of the Local Government Board for the purpose of concentrating all local measures of assistance, and making grants out of the funds placed at their disposal by the government. It is not implied that the Emergency Committee is to be superseded, and I feel sure that its members will continue to render their splendid and invaluable services with the new committee in looking after the welfare and comfort of the people. The great difficulty which we are experiencing is to find suitable house for the homeless. There are few, if any, available, and I fear that it may be necessary for many of the people to leave the district, at any rate temporarily, although very effort is being made to find accommodation as far as possible in the borough.

In conclusion, may I say once more how deeply indebted I am to the numerous ladies and gentlemen attached to the various Institutes for the splendid way in which they placed themselves at the disposal of the people, and for their unstinted efforts on their behalf? I shall hope at a more convenient time to meet them all again.

I regret to say that the time at my disposal has not given me an opportunity of going outside the district, but I have visited the local hospitals, and I am glad to say that from all the accounts which I have heard form the others, most of the injured are progressing well.

(signed) R. Mansfield, Mayor.
dated 26th January, 1917.

Major Carthew's Sympathy

The copy of the 'Stratford Express' containing details of the terrible disaster in a munition factory in the East end of London only reached me just now, but I shall be glad if you will allow me to express, through the columns of your widely read paper, my sincere and deep sympathy with the sufferers in this great tragedy. Thanks to the Germanic Powers, who precipitated this orgy of blood out here, those of us who serve have become accustomed to sights of suffering and death on the battlefield, but it seems a hundred times more terrible when these things happen so far away from the shock of war, and involve so many helpless women and children. Accidents of this kind, so immense and so staggering, bring home to us out here the risks run day by day by all the thousands in England whose names never appear in our honours list or are 'mentioned in dispatches,' but without whose hard and often dangerous work the Boche could not be beaten. The whole district seems to have responded magnificently to the call for help for the homeless, and I should very much have liked to have helped in the only other way possible if one could not have been there oneself, but I see that the Mayor has decided it is better not to open a fund. I can only, therefore, express to those who are bereaved, and to the sufferers, an expression of sympathy, which is, believe me, very genuine.

(signed) THOMAS CARTHEW
1st Wing R.F.C.,
B.E.F., France.

Seamen's Hospital's Thanks to Workers

Permit me, through your columns, to express our warmest thanks to all those ladies and gentlemen who so kindly came to the aid of the Seamen's Hospital on the night of the explosion. Many kind friends rendered great assistance, but it was not possible to personally thank them, and some left without even their names being known. Over 200 patients were treated; many of them, after first-aid, were able to return to their homes, but many were retained in the wards, and unhappily some died during the night. I merely mention these facts to give you an idea of the pressure there was on the hospital, and the value of the kind assistance rendered.

(signed) P. MICHELLI, Secretary.

P.S. – My committee, at their last meeting, passed a vote of sympathy with all those who were injured, and with the friends and relatives of those who lost their lives owing to the great explosion.

Catholics and the Explosion Victims

On Sunday there was a large attendance at Saint Margaret's and All Saints' Church, at a High Mass (sung by the Rev. O. Fitzgerald) for the victims of the explosion; and on Wednesday a special service was held in the same church. A number of the sufferers have been accommodated in St. Margaret's Schoolrooms, and the Rev. J. Dempsey has worked untiringly on their behalf.

Free Churches and the Explosion

At the joint meeting of all the free churches of south West Ham, held in Plaistow Congregational Church on Thursday last, a resolution was passed expressing heartfelt sympathy with the people in that district of East London who are distressed and bereaved by the recent terrible disaster. It is the wish of the Churches that any ability they possess may be used in the service of the desolate sufferers. They are glad to have been able to place at the disposal of the needy such rooms and resources as they had to offer, and they unitedly pray that mourners may find human and divine comfort.

Arethusa Training Ship for Orphans

The National Refugees and their Arethusa training ship, of 164, Shaftesbury Avenue, W.C., will receive any boys or girls between the ages of 5 and 13½ into their Homes and boys into their ship if of suitable age, who have been rendered fatherless by the explosion. No votes are needed and no outfits are required, nor any payment to be made by the widows.

Volunteers' Help

In the special police services during the past week the Ilford, Chadwell Heath, Barking, East Ham, Forest Gate, Plaistow, North Woolwich, and West Ham Sub-divisions of the Special Constabulary have been particularly prominent. Their ordinary rounds of duty at the different police stations have also been attended to as usual.

The West Ham Sub-Division are short of men, and gentlemen wishing to volunteer for this special class of 'work' may apply for enrolment any evening. Candidates must be over military age.

SATURDAY 10 FEBRUARY 1917

The Explosion
Resumed Inquests – Survivors' Accounts of the Disaster

The inquiry into the death of victims of the explosion was resumed by the local coroner on Monday morning. Inquests were held on 53 bodies, of whom 19 were under 20 years of age and ten under 10 years of age.

Major T.H. Crozier, H.M. Inspector of Explosives appeared for the Home Office; Mr. H.M. Cohen for the Ministry of Munitions and the National Union of Gasworkers was represented by Mr. L. Bingham. Many of the witnesses wore surgical bandages.

The names of the victims were:-

John Howard, 36; Frederick Charles Sell, 45; Henry Vickers, 49; John Royal Howard, 21; Frederick Gustav Craft, 36; Harold Foster, 21; Hugh McMarth, 24; Ernest Arthur Jenkins, 34; John Walter Enness, 25; Henry George Lidbury, 69; William Gray, 39; Thomas Henry Acton, 62; Henry Rogers, 23; Mary Wass, 32; Elsie Wass, 10; Charles Hiscock, 45; Thomas Oates, 8; Stanley Wass, 13; Willam Patrick, 9; Ruby Patrick, 5; Rose Patrick, 3; Edward Foreshaw, 30; Jeffrey J.T. Wainwright, 17; Thomas Tasker, 53; Ellen Boyce, 32; Alfred Edward Harlow, 39; Lizzie Lawence, 16; Lillian B. Davey, 15; Edward Godsmark, 15; Elizabeth Preston, 28; Dorothy Preston, 11 months; Catherine Smith, 16; Henry Badcock, 26; Hugh McCoombs, 44; May Gertrude Jennings, 20; Robert William Greenleaf, 17; Ellen Frances Jane Noakes, 20; Sidney Joseph Benstead, 26; John George Chandler, 27; William Lambert, 34; Walter Mauger, 26; James Henry Reeve, 44; Ethel Elmer Betts, 4 months; Edward James Kidd, 49; David Taylor, 69; Francis C.L. Simpson, 50; Roydon S. Patrick, 23 months; George. E. Wenborn, 49; Walter Ernest Sharp, 36; Norman W. Gardner, 5; James Bruce, 61; George Erick Preston, 3½; George Henry Hopkins, 24.

The first witness called was Mrs Sarah Ann Hopkins who stated that her son, George Henry Hopkins, was a chemical worker employed at the factory. She now identified a head as that of her son, a married man.

P.S. Randall, 92K, said at 7.13 a.m. on the 19th ult., he found the body of fireman Fredk. Sell which had been blown through a fence. The top of his head was off.

Samuel Betts, station officer of the fire brigade in the neighbourhood of the factory, said he received a call about 7 o'clock. They got out the engine and it was placed against the gate of the factory. They were all busy getting the fire engine to work, and the factory was then 'well alight'.

The Coroner: 'Did the explosion occur soon after you got there?' – 'About five minutes.'

'Was the place alight when you got there?' – 'It was what we should call in a brigade phrase "well alight".'

Juror: 'Was the call by telephone or message?' – 'I could not say, but I understand that a lad did call. I was not in the station itself at the time, but in my apartments adjoining. The fireman Vickers was at work with the engine.'

The Coroner: 'You were rendered unconscious yourself weren't you?' – 'Yes: I had one engine at work, and was striving to get the second delivery when – I don't remember any more.'

P.S. Randall said the body of Betts was lying alongside that of Sell. He did not see the bodies of any other firemen.

Stephen Arthur Barton, an engine driver and charge hand in the employ of the Port of London Authority, said they were just knocking off work. He was paying off the men when the explosion occurred, but he had seen the fire about five minutes before. The next thing they heard was the explosion and the office was blown on the top of them. In answer to the cries of 'Help' witness went to the assistance of John Royal Howard, a bargeman. Witness had not seen the deceased before the explosion. He was knocking off work at the time, and would have finished in a few minutes.

The Coroner: 'Was he conscious?' – 'Oh yes.'

Charles Price, barge attendant to the Port of London Authority, said he was standing at the door of a fitters shop some distance from the factory.

The Coroner: 'Were you watching the fire?' – 'Yes, I have seen the place alight quite a dozen times during the last fifteen years. It is a small purifier at the side of the works, I take it.'

'Then you were not alarmed?' – 'No.' 'Whilst you were watching the explosion occurred?' – 'Yes.' 'With the result that you were blown back into the shop, and the deceased man Howard was knocked down?' – 'Yes, sir.'

Witness said that he went to Howard's assistance and found a large piece of boiler plate lying beside him. His legs were injured and he was bleeding profusely. He was conscious and witness assisted to take him to the hospital.

Witness was pressed to as to the last time a fire occurred at the factory, but he could not say even to a year.

The Coroner: 'Has there been a fire there during the last six months?' – 'I can't say that.'

A juror expressed his opinion that it was a very unsatisfactory statement to make seeing that the witness could give no details. Another juror: 'Were any special precautions taken to prevent these fires?'

The Coroner: 'Do you know anything about the works? Have you ever been inside them?' – 'No.' 'Do you know what purifiers are?' – 'Not in any particular. I don't.'

A solicitor who appeared for the relatives of the deceased elicited the fact that the 'purifier' was some distance from the main building.

William James Copland, superintendent under the P.L.A., said the deceased, Harold Foster, was a assistant pay clerk under him. He was single. The deceased was on duty at the time of the explosion, but witness was not.

Vernon Charles Roberts, labourer employed by the P.L.A., said he was with Harold Foster and others watching the fire from some distance off. Witness and deceased walked towards a gate about 300 yards from the factory. They reached the gate and were still watching the fire when the explosion occurred.

The Coroner: 'Did you see Foster fall?' – 'No sir, I saw him start running.' 'You gave this information to the police as to where his body might be found?' – 'Yes sir.' 'And it was recovered the next morning?' – 'Yes.'

P.C. Bloomfield, P.L.A. Police, said on the morning following the explosion he found the body of the deceased man Foster among the debris of a shed. This shed had not been burned but blown down.

Herbert James Shipton, a mechanical engineers foreman employed by the P.L.A., said he left his shop about ten minutes before the explosion.

The Coroner: 'You did not feel the effects of the explosion?' – 'I did, but was not hurt.' 'You returned about eight o'clock?' – 'Yes, and I saw the body of Ernest Arthur Jenkins, who was working at one of the workshops.'

In reply to further questions, witness said that the deceased had been into the blacksmiths shop, and was returning when the explosion occurred. He should have ceased work at 7.50.

Alfred William Wilton, a fitters labourer, employed by the P.L.A., said he did not see the fire before the explosion. Witness was blown off his feet by the explosion, and when he recovered he heard cries for help. He then found that the door of the shop had been blown out of its socket, and on lifting up the door he found Jenkins lying underneath. He was unconscious and had a large wound on the top of his head. He was taken on a barrow to the hospital.

Dr. Kennedy was then called with regard to a girl named Catherine Smith, aged 16. He said she was burned practically all over the body. She lived until 8 a.m. on the 22nd, and then died from shock following the burns.

John Peel, a foreman in the grain department at the dock, said he was in the office at he time. He saw the fire before the explosion and was in the company of the deceased Henry George Lidbury, looking at it.

The Coroner: 'You rather anticipated that an explosion would occur?' – 'Yes, sir, I did.' 'And Lidbury spoke about the money?' – 'Yes.'

He left me to go into the inner office, and just then the explosion occurred and he was knocked down. He was about to pay off the gang. Witness added that he was rendered unconscious by the explosion, but was now getting better.

A Juror: 'Was the fire a large one?' – 'The flames seemed to be running up the tower.' 'Could you identify where the fire was?' – 'No. But we knew the factory.'

Arthur Swaine, permanent labourer in the bulk grain department of the Port of London Authority, said he was about to enter one of the doors when the explosion occurred, and he was blown about 20 yards along the passage. His shoulder was hurt, but he was otherwise uninjured. He assisted in the search and found Lidbury's body. He was then apparently quite dead, and witness helped to carry the body to the police box.

A Juror: 'Did you see the factory on fire before the explosion?' – 'Yes, and I called out "For God's sake, run. The stuff is alight." '

Aaron George, chief engineer at the flour mill which was damaged, said he was at home at the time of the explosion. The deceased William Gray was employed as a stationary engine driver at the mill. After the explosion witness returned to the mill, and tried to find Gray, but failed to do so.

The Coroner: 'Your house was wrecked, but you were not injured?' – 'Well I had to attend to myself before I could go up to the mill.'

George Tree, a stoker, said he last saw Gray at 6.45 when the latter called his attention to the fire. Witness went down to the stoke-hole and left Gray. 'I never saw him after that,' witness added.

Albert Edward Ottley, a stoker at the flour mill, said he was on duty at the time of the disaster. Witness was in the stoke-hole, and saw the deceased coming downstairs. At that time the explosion occurred and witness was blown out of the stoke-hole. After pulling himself together witness went outside, and found the deceased lying between the quay and the mill. The last words he said were 'Stop the engine'.

Mrs. Emily Patson said her father, Thomas Henry Acton, had left off work at 5 o'clock on the 19th ult. He was going upstairs when he saw the fire, and called attention to it. He then went out to try and render assistance, and witness never saw him alive again. P.S. Randall said he found the body of the deceased man Acton, a few yards from the fire engine. He was lying dead in the roadway.

Alfred Doyle, a foreman at the destroyed factory, said Henry Rogers, the deceased, was under him. He was employed from 2 till 10, and witness last saw him alive in the afternoon. Witness was not there at the time of the explosion. The Coroner said there was a difficulty in ascertaining who actually found the body of Rogers. It was taken to the mortuary, and was probably found by the military in the course of their search.

Constable Groom, 945 K, said that at 5.20 p.m. on the 20th he saw the body of a man believed to be Charles Hiscock, an engineer, at a private house. Witness took charge of the body, and conveyed it to a mortuary.

Mrs. Catherine Oates, wife of a labourer, said the deceased child Stanley Thomas Oates was eight years of age. On the evening in question she was at home with her six children when she saw the fire. After the explosion witness ran into the street with her five children, but missed the boy Tommy. Witness subsequently borrowed a candle and returned to the house, where she found the lad lying in the passage. A large piece of iron had come through the roof and was lying on the body of the boy. Her daughter Catherine had one of her arms cut off, apparently by the same piece of iron.

James Abbot, a labourer said that at 6.40 he went to a garage in the vicinity to watch the fire. In the garage was a plumber named Edward Foreshaw, and he ran towards the fire. The explosion occurred, and witness was thrown down, and when he picked himself up there was no sign of Foreshaw.

Charles Bell, a clerk, said he last saw Geoffrey James Thomas Wainwright, an assistant wage clerk, a couple of minutes before the explosion. Witness and the deceased worked at an adjoining factory, and two office cleaners ran in and told them of the fire. Witness looked out, and realised the danger, and called to the deceased and another lad who had ran out. They did not answer. Witness collected up some petty cash, and just then the explosion occurred, and the ceiling began to fall. 'I ran into the safe,' added witness, 'and when the second explosion occurred I remember no more. The next morning I saw Wainwright's scalp at the foot of the stairs.'

James Preston, a rollerman employed at the flour mill, said he was on duty on the Friday night. His wife, Elizabeth Preston, would have been at home. The only one he could speak with certainty about was his son Eric. The probability was that the child Dorothy was with her mother at the time.

Albert Edward Harlow, a boy of about twelve years of age, said his father's name was Alfred Edward Harlow. He was a hawker, and was delivering oil in the district at the time of the explosion. Afterwards witness did not see his father again, but he (witness) escaped.

Charles Hill, foreman at the adjoining factory, said the deceased man Henry Badcock was employed under his direction. His body had been recovered, but witness was unable to say where from.

The witness Doyle, recalled, said the deceased Hugh McCoombs was also employed at the destroyed factory. Witness had not been able to ascertain where his body was found.

Mabel Ann Hudson, a domestic servant employed at the wood factory, said she was with a young woman named Ellen Noakes who was employed as a cook. The latter told witness and her sister, who was also present, that the munition factory was on fire. She said 'What shall we do?' and witness said 'I am going to get my boots and go home.' Witness and her sister started to leave, but the explosion occurred almost immediately, and the place fell in on them. Witness was injured, but did not lose consciousness, and she called to the deceased, but got no answer. The kitchen in which Miss Noakes was when witness left was cut off, and witness and her sister 'got away down a drain pipe and through another window.'

Sidney Charles Cole, a gatekeeper at a neighbouring factory, said that on the following morning he heard that Ellen Noakes was missing. He searched the factory, and found her in the passage leading to the mess-room. She was dead.

Mr. Doyle, recalled, said the deceased Joseph Sidney Benstead was another man employed at the munition factory. Witness could not ascertain where his body was found.

George Cartwright, a dining-room proprietor, said the deceased Lily Davy, aged 15, was a servant employed by him. She called his attention to the fact that a fire was taking place. A few minutes later she left to go home, and that was the last time he saw her alive.

The Coroner: 'Was your shop damaged?' – 'Yes, very much.'

George Bruce, a labourer employed at the munition factory, said he was working with John George Chandler and four other men on the soda crystal plant, which was about 25 yards away from the other plant.

The Coroner: 'What did you first see or hear?' – 'I heard a noise as though someone had dropped a big sheet of corrugated iron. I looked out of the window, and saw the plant was afire.' 'What did you do?' – 'Well, the other four men went away down the river, and Chandler and I remained where we were and watched the flames for a few seconds. Then we made off up the river.' Witness added that Chandler exclaimed 'Look at the flames! Let's go back and see if we can help.' They started back towards the factory, but by that time the flames were very fierce. Witness advised Chandler to turn back again, and at that moment the explosion occurred. Witness was thrown down, and part of the roof fell on him. 'After things had stopped falling,' pursued witness, 'I found that I could wriggle out of it. I walked into a pit of liquor, and afterwards found myself in a field. There was no trace of Chandler at that time.'

The Coroner: 'How far away from the factory were you at the time of the explosion?' – 'About 75 to 80 yards.'

Dr. Wilson said the deceased Robert William Greenleaf was admitted to the hospital very badly burned. He died on Sunday afternoon from shock following burns.

Edward James Kidd was also admitted to the hospital the same evening. He was suffering from a wound behind the knee. He was operated on and appeared to be getting on well, but took a turn and died. Death was due to the injuries following the explosion.

The witness Doyle, recalled, said the deceased William Lambert was employed at the munition factory. Witness could not find out how his body was recovered.

Hetty Sands, a married woman, said that on the night in question she was working in the lift in the factory. About 6.35 she went to see the deceased Walter Mauger, a labourer about some work. With permission she left the place with Mrs. Randall. Whilst away they heard two reports, and Mrs. Randall then pointed out that the place was alight. The last time she saw the deceased he was at his place at the top of the lift.

The Coroner: 'Was there any fire on the lift?' – 'No, sir – none whatever.'

Doyle, recalled, said the deceased James Henry Reeve, was a labourer at the works.

Frederick Blenheim, assistant works chemist, said that shortly after the fire broke out he saw Reeve and Sharp. They were connecting up some fire hose that belonged to the firm.

The Coroner: 'You told them to run?' – 'Yes. I felt it my duty. I told them it was a question of running for their lives, but I suppose they thought it was their duty to have a go for it.' 'You never saw them again?' – 'No.' Witness also spoke of seeing David Taylor, aged 69, a watchman, employed near the plant. 'I told him to run for his life,' said witness, 'but he was very bad on his feet, and had not much chance.'

Henry John Hough said a watchman named Francis Charles Leonard Simpson had directions to go to the oil wharf next to the munition factory to watch some barges. He was one of the victims of the explosion.

Harold Peterson, a works foreman at a factory, said that at 6.30 he saw the deceased with his son. They spoke about a barge moored at the wharf, and whilst so doing he heard a hissing noise

like the fusing of a electric wire. Witness went outside the gate-
house, and found the munition factory was on fire. The top story
was then well alight. Witness told Simpson to get out as soon as
possible, and witness went in to see his 'guv'nor.'

The Coroner: 'Was he in the house at the time?' – 'es. I rushed in
and got him out.'

Inspr. Vernon said he was on duty at the ruins of the factory on
the Sunday morning, and saw four trunks recovered from the
debris. They were removed to the temporary mortuaries, and were
subsequently identified as the bodies of James Bruce, Dr. Andrea
Angel, Catherine Hogg, and Francis Simpson. A doctor said the
deceased child Elsie Wass was unconscious and had severe injuries
to her head and body; she died without recovering consciousness.
John Royal Howard was suffering compound fractures of both
legs, and he died the same night. John Enness was suffering from
compound fractures of the leg and, he died the following morning.
Ernest Jenkins had a compound fracture of the leg and a scalp
wound, and he died the following morning. William Gray had
burns all over the body and he died the following morning. In each
case death was due to shock following the injuries.

Henry Blackman, a cooper formerly employed at the works, said
the deceased Walter Ernest Sharp was his labourer. Just before seven
o'clock witness saw workmen running from the factory, and
Wenborn ran towards Dr. Angel's room. Witness did not see Sharp
alive again.

Margaret Mitchell said just before seven o'clock she was at the
cottage adjoining the factory, preparing Dr. Angel's dinner. Mr.
Wenborn came to the door of the cottage and shouted in an agitated manner to Dr. Angel. The latter came downstairs and ran
towards the factory. Witness opened the back door and saw that the
factory was on fire, and she did not see Mr. Wenborn alive again.

The Coroner: 'Did you see Mr. Angel?' – 'I just saw him going
over to the plant.'

Dr. Brews told the Coroner that he had examined a charred
body, which was headless and without arms or legs. It was the body

of a young female under 23 years of age.

The Coroner: 'Was the body very much charred?' – 'Yes, sir, very much, most of the organs were destroyed by fire.' 'You could not determine very much then?' – 'No, sir, I was able to determine the sex beyond all doubt, but except that it was a young person I could find out nothing.'

Mrs. Rathlin said that at the time of the accident she was staying with her sister, Mrs. Gardner. She was watching the fire with Mr. Gardner, and when the explosion occurred the house collapsed. Subsequently she saw the body of Norman Gardner, her sister's son. The child was taken out of the ruins of the house by his father. At the time he was alive and was taken to the hospital.

Mr. Blenheim, said the deceased James Bruce was a watchman in the employ of the firm, and after the fire had started witness saw this man open the gates in order that firemen might get the hose through. The engine did not pass though the gates, but he believed they had made one connection when the explosion occurred. The last time witness saw the deceased he was going into the office.

Alfred Lawrence, a coal porter said the deceased Catherine Hogg was his foster daughter and was 16 years old last August. She was a factory hand, and worked on the top floor of the munition factory. She was on the 2 to 10 p.m. shift on the day in question. She was known at the factory as Lizzie Lawrence. She wore two rings on her hand.

The Coroner: 'You have seen the charred remains? You can't identify them of course?' – 'No, sir, but I was told about the rings by the doctor.' Mrs. Sands said she last saw Lizzie Lawrence at the top of the lift. Her work was to send down the crude material to put in the melting pot. The Coroner said the body of Lizzie Lawrence, in respect of whom Dr. Brew had given evidence, was the only one not properly identified. The other girls working there had been accounted for, and the jury would probably have no difficulty in finding that this was her body.

Thomas Mileham, a cartage contractor, said that on the Sunday afternoon he was with the mother of Hugh McMarth. The gable end of a house had collapsed, and witness asked the military to search among the debris. They did so, and the body of McMarth was recovered.

Herbert Mills, a foreman at the flour mill, said John Walter Ennes was a motor driver employed in connection with the flour mill. The last time witness saw him alive he had just stepped off his wagon. He was picked up about 80 or 100 yards away from the wagon.

Arthur Brown, a flour mill clerk, said he saw Enness, who was then semi-conscious. He was placed on a tug and taken to hospital. The inquiry was adjourned for three weeks.

Funeral of Police Hero

On Saturday the funeral took place, at East Finchley, of P.C. Greenoff, who lost his life in the great explosion. He did his utmost to keep people back from the fire. He was warning them that there was likely to be an explosion when it occurred, and he was knocked down and received injuries from which he died. At the inquest it was stated that several people owed their lives to his timely warning. A great number of the regular and special police forces were present. A large contingent of men and officers were present from the 'K' Division under Supt. Boxhall, and the 'specials' were under Sergt. Fowell. The long procession was headed by an advance guard, under Inspr. E. Brennan, composed of Police-constables Chaffee, Carpenter, Coalbran, Dadson, Davidson, Fisher, Hodgson, Lincoln, Shopland, Sargent, Seal and Taylor. Then came the band of the 'K' Division, and the hearse and private mourners. The cortege was met at the cemetery gates by Sir Edward R . Henry, G.C.V.O., Commissioner; Major Sir E.F. Wodehouse, K.C.V.O., C.B., Assistant Commissioner of the Metropolitan Police; and the Rev. G.H. Mitchell (Chaplain to the Mariners Friends Society). At the burial ground an impressive scene was witnessed, the procession forming a huge square around the grave. The

Rev. G.H. Mitchell paid a high tribute to the dead hero. The Commissioner of Police has received the following letter from the King's Private Secretary :-

The King is grieved to hear that Police-constable George Greenoff, through whose self-sacrificing efforts many lives were saved after the recent explosion at a munitions factory near London, has died from his injuries. I am commanded to ask you to convey to his widow and family His Majesty's sincere sympathy, and to assure you of the King's sense of admiration that the best traditions of the police have been nobly maintained in this signal act of courage and devotion to duty.

Forest Gate Ratepayers' Association

The monthly meeting of the Forest Gate Ratepayers' Association was held at Earlham Hall on Monday evening. Mr. H. Hulbert (Vice-chairman) presided, supported by the hon. secretary (Mr. J. Park) and the hon. financial secretary (Mr. J. MacCarthy)

The Explosion

The Chairman remarked as this was the first meeting of the Association since the terrible explosion, he thought they should place on record their sympathy with the bereaved and injured.

This was agreed to, and it was decided to send a resolution to the Town Clerk.

Mr. Nathan said that various sums of money had been sent to the Mayor for the use of the people affected by the explosion, and also a quantity of clothing and other gifts in kind. In matters of this kind, where people out of their sympathy gave presents, he thought it only right that a statement should be published, so that donors might know that their money had been properly dealt with.

The Chairman said he understood that the Ministry of Munitions had agreed to take over the whole of the responsibility, both financial and personal, and he did not think that the voluntary subscriptions would amount to very much.

Councillor Wordley said the Mayor had received several amounts, but the Minister of Munitions had stated that there must be no published statement with reference to them. The Ministry had undertaken full responsibility, and would reimburse people who had suffered loss, and pay for the funerals of the victims. They would also undertake the repairing of rebuilding work necessary. This work was promptly put in hand, and by the end of this week they would have 200 of the partly demolished houses again fit for habitation. About 800 people were rendered homeless, and the great difficulty was to provide homes for them. They were very particular as to where they went. Those out of work had, upon the instructions of the Ministry of Munitions, been given first chance of employment at the Arsenal. The Councillor went on to say that so much clothing had been sent in that they had to take an empty shop for the purpose of storing it. There was probably sufficient clothing to provide all the people with twice as much as they had been used to. At a special meeting of the Works Committee of the Town Council that day the Ministry of Munitions had stated that they preferred to rebuild the fire station, because the Minister of Works believed that he would be able to commandeer material and labour, and get the place put up very much more quickly than the Council could hope to do.

Mr. Ward said it would be impossible to issue any financial statement, because people called in at the hall and 'left money with almost anybody there'.

Manufacturers' Recognition of Helpers

At a largely attended meeting of East London manufacturers held yesterday, it was unanimously agreed that some recognition of the services rendered by the various hospitals and other organisations to the maimed and wounded, as well as those who worked so arduously in rescue work, should be made in such a form as will show our appreciation of such services by the firms interested, and we were appointed to carry the necessary arrangements.

We propose that the individual subscriptions should be limited to £100, and, as already five firms have promised these amounts, we shall be pleased to bear by return of post, if possible, what amount may be subscribed.

C.E. LEO LYLE (Abram Lyle and Sons, Ltd.)

JAMES BOYD (James Keiller and Sons, Ltd.)

JOHN W. HOPE (John Knight, Ltd.)
Royal Primrose Soap Works,
London, E.
7th February, 1917

Sympathy with the Sufferers

Resolutions of sympathy and condolence with the sufferers and the bereaved have been received from:-

The London Outdoor Staff of the Prudential Assurance Co. Ltd.
Poplar Board of Guardians.
Ilford Branch National Union of Railwaymen.
Edmonton Urban District Council.
Executive Committee, Central Hackney Liberal and Radical Association.
Free Churches of South West Ham.
Hackney United Friendly Hospital and Philanthropic Society.
Representative Managers of L.C.C. Elementary Schools.
Independent Order of Oddfellows, Manchester.
Unity Friendly Society, Stepney District.

Wood Green Allotments Federation.

Loyal Pride of Essex Lodge, Independent Order of Oddfellows.

Fetter Lane Men's Meeting.

Borough of Poplar Trades Council.

Welfare Committee, Edward Cook and Co. Ltd.

London County Council.

Deptford Metropolitan Borough Council.

Leyton, No. 2. Branch, National Union of Railwaymen.

Association of Professional Fire Brigade Officers.

The Principal, Staff and Pupils of the Water Lane Higher
    Elementary School.

Croydon Fire Brigade Committee.

The Premier of the Dominion of New Zealand.

Metropolitan Essex District of the London Congregational
    Union.

The Mayor of East Ham.

Poplar No. 1. Branch, National Union of Railwaymen.

Tottenham Urban District Council.

Barking Town Urban District Council.

National Union of Vehicle Workers.

Greengate Congregational Church.

East Ham Town Council.

Southwark Borough Council.

King and Queen in Explosion Area

The Court Circular of February 4th, contained the following
announcement :-

'Their Majesties and the Princess Mary, attended by
Commander Sir Charles Cust, Bart, R.N., visited this afternoon
the district of the recent explosion in the neighbourhood of
London, and subsequently saw a number of the injured in the
London Hospital and the Poplar Hospital.

EXPLOSION OF T.N.T. AT SILVERTOWN.

REPORT

OF THE

COMMITTEE

APPOINTED BY THE

RIGHT HONOURABLE THE SECRETARY OF STATE FOR THE HOME DEPARTMENT

TO INQUIRE INTO

THE CAUSE OF THE EXPLOSION WHICH OCCURRED ON FRIDAY, 19TH JANUARY 1917, AT THE CHEMICAL WORKS OF MESSRS. BRUNNER, MOND AND COMPANY, LIMITED, CRESCENT WHARF, SILVERTOWN IN THE COUNTY OF ESSEX.

1 9 1 7.

WARRANT OF APPOINTMENT

I hereby appoint

Sir ERNLEY BLACKWELL, K.C.B., Assistant Under-Secretary of State
Major A. McNEILL COOPER-KEY, C.B., H.M. Chief Inspector of Explosives,
and
Colonel Sir FREDERIC L. NATHAN,

to be a Committee to inquire and report as to the cause of the explosion which occurred on Friday, 19th January, at the Chemical Works of Messrs Brunner, Mond and Company, Limited, Crescent Wharf, Silvertown, and the circumstances connected therewith, and to make any recommendations which appear to be desirable.

I further appoint Sir ERNLEY BLACKWELL to be Chairman and Mr. P. TAINSH to be Secretary to the Committee.

(Signed) Geo. Cave

Home Office, Whitehall, S.W.,
23rd January 1917.

REPORT

To the Right Hon. Sir GEORGE CAVE, K.C., M.P., His Majesty's Principal Secretary of State for the Home Department.

Sir,

In pursuance of your instructions dated 23rd January 1917, we have held an Inquiry into the cause of the explosion which occurred on January 19th, 1917, at the factory belonging to Messrs Brunner, Mond & Co., Ltd, situated at Crescent Wharf, Silvertown, and the circumstances connected therewith.

In the course of our Inquiry we examined a number of witnesses, and a list of these, together with their qualifications, is given in appendix I.

We now beg to report as follows:-

Description of the Factory.

The area known as the Crescent Wharf (see Plan A) is approximately rectangular in shape, 400 yards from north to south, and 130 yards from east to west at its widest part. It is bounded on the north by a goods line of the Great Eastern Railway which runs parallel to and adjoining the North Woolwich Road, on the south by the River Thames, on the east by the oil depot of Silvertown Lubricants, Ltd, and on the west by the 'Vanesta' Works.

On the further side of the North Woolwich Road there were several blocks of dwelling houses, the local fire station and two important flour mills. The situation of the works in fact was, from the point of view of explosives manufacture, extremely bad, and in normal times it is certain that no such work would have been undertaken on these premises.

The building in which the process of purifying T.N.T. was carried on was situate at the northern end of the premises, and is coloured red upon the plan. The plant in this building had been

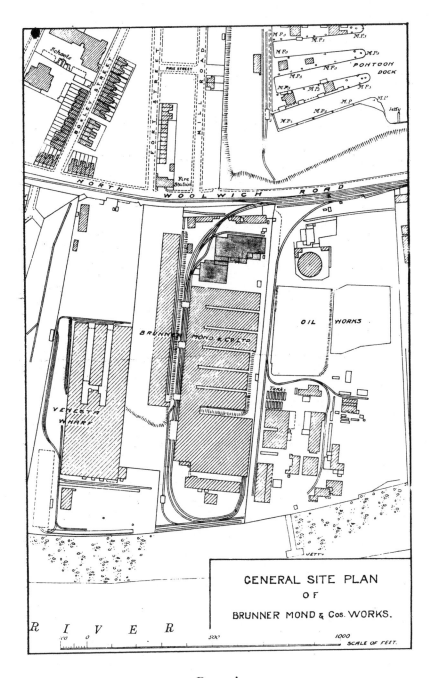

GENERAL SITE PLAN
OF
BRUNNER MOND & Cos. WORKS.

PLAN A.

formerly used for the manufacture of caustic soda but it had lain idle as a stand-by plant for five years prior to June 1915, when it was decided to adapt it for the purification of T.N.T.

Upon the remainder of the premises, down to the river frontage, the crystallisation of sodium carbonate was carried on, and continued to be carried on after the purification of T.N.T. at the northern end of the premises was commenced in September 1915. The circumstances in which, owing to the exigencies of the war, it was decided that, in spite of the general unsuitability of the site, it was essential in the national interest that certain operations in connection with the supply of T.N.T. should be carried on in this factory were fully described to us by Lord Moulton in the following words:-

Early in the year 1915 we found our capacity for purifying T.N.T. insufficient for the probable task which would be thrown upon it. I had come to the conclusion that I would not allow the makers of T.N.T. to set up purifying works in their factories. The dangers of making T.N.T. are comparatively small, and are of a totally different type to the dangers from purifying, and I felt convinced that in order to protect my output I ought not to allow purifying works to be put up in the same place as manufacturing works....

We had established a place at Rainham which was well removed from any habitation and was suitable in every way for the purpose of purifying crude T.N.T., but that was obviously insufficient, and the other supplies were clearly too small if the artillerists insisted on having purified T.N.T. for their charges, whether mixed or unmixed with nitrate of ammonia. The consequence was we had to look about for some method of promptly meeting this deficiency. I heard, I think from a member of the firm Messrs. Chance & Hunt, that these works at Silvertown were standing idle, and that they were the only works which he knew of which were capable of being adapted to a method of purification which was not recrystallisation, but was a method of washing in hot alcohol.... Accordingly, we communicated with Messrs. Brunner, Mond &

Co., and although there was no formal commandeering of the works – because Messrs. Brunner, Mond & Co. have always met our wishes so willingly and so energetically – yet practically we requisitioned those works, and put them into the hands of Brunner, Mond & Co., as our agents to adapt them to this process of purification. They did so, and if I remember rightly, it was about September 1915, that they commenced to work, and they have worked ever since until the explosion. They have turned out about 10 tons a day, that is, 70 tons a week. They have been visited by my Inspectors, and not only by my Inspectors, but by the heads of the branch of the Department which takes charge of contracts and takes charge of these particular factories, and we have always felt that they were in extremely good hands. We had very great faith in Dr Lamb; and the experts at the head of the establishment of Messrs. Brunner, Mond & Co. I know also visited them. So the employment of these works for this purpose was practically by the orders of my Department. We could see no other way of obtaining purifying works within the time that they were necessary....

I desire to say this, because I wish to make quite plain the part played by Brunner, Mond & Co. in this matter. It was we who required them to let us have these disused works, and we who employed them to adapt to the new use and to carry it on.

In reply to the question 'Was there any reason for keeping these works on?' Lord Moulton stated: 'I did not feel it safe to discontinue them, because even now the requirements of the artillerists in the way of T.N.T. are perfectly uncertain....The actual amount that may be demanded of what I may call purified T.N.T. for the purpose of charges – that is to say not exploders and not fuses, because for those we can easily do it – but for the actual bursting charges it remains doubtful, and if extreme views prevail, we shall have all our work cut out for us in order to get sufficient. Therefore I have never felt safe in discontinuing Silvertown which was doing its work very well, and I believed and still believe was in very good hands.'

The whole of the work of purifying the T.N.T. was carried out in the one building, the crude material and the finished product being kept under the same roof. As already indicated in Lord Moulton's statement very little alteration was required to adapt the caustic soda plant to the T.N.T. purification process, the principal constructional addition being the erection at the top of the building of the corrugated iron structure described later.

The plant was thoroughly scraped and washed, and the building itself washed down in an endeavour to get rid of all traces of alkali. It must be recognised, however, that this would not be easy of accomplishment, and, as a matter of fact Dr. Lamb, in his evidence, stated that for some weeks after the commencement of operations the colour of the mother liquors indicated that some traces of alkali remained.

Under their contract with the Ministry, Messrs. Brunner, Mond & Co. received a commission of 5s. per ton of purified T.N.T. produced, the whole cost of production being borne by the Ministry. Upon a production of 3,000 tons this would represent a profit to the company of 750l. per annum, but as they, on their own account, specially engaged Dr. Angel to superintend the process at a salary of 400l., and increased the salary of the Works Manager, the actual profit was reduced to a merely nominal sum.

Arrangements for Protection of the Factory.

The main entrance to the Crescent Wharf premises was in the North Woolwich Road, and all employees entering were checked there by a doorkeeper. About 286 persons were employed upon the premises altogether, but of these only 63 were actually employed in the T.N.T. building working three shifts of 21 in each. The entrance to the T.N.T. building was by a door facing the North Woolwich Road, and here again was a doorkeeper who was well acquainted with all persons employed in the building and would have easily recognised and stopped an intruder. The T.N.T. building was effectively shut off from the rest of the premises, either by the walls of the building itself or by a corrugated iron fence topped with barbed wire.

The external protection of the premises was, at the date of the explosion, vested in the Metropolitan Police, and we are satisfied that their arrangements were adequate. We think that it is in the highest degree improbable that any unauthorised person was or could have been upon the premises on the evening in question.

In recruiting labour for the new work the firm employed, as far as they could, all their old hands, trusted men, some of whom had been with them for 20 years. They took on, as far as possible, workers who were known to their own men, and they distributed their old hands through the three shifts so as to leaven each shift with men whom they knew could be relied upon. As statements have appeared in the press with regard to the employment of enemy aliens at these works, we caused careful inquiry to be made with regard to this matter. We found that there were no alien enemies employed in the T.N.T. building, and only one on the rest of the premises. This man is a German, aged 57, who has been in this country for 47 years. He is married to a British born wife, and he has 12 British born children living, three of whom are serving in the army. He is a man of very good character, and had been exempted from internment and repatriation upon advice of the Advisory Committee. He had never been inside the T.N.T. plant, and on the night of the explosion he went home about 6 p.m. to see a son who had just returned on leave from the front. No suspicion of any kind attaches to this man.

Description of the Process.

Many of the operations cannot conceivably have had anything to do with the accident, so that a general description of the process will suffice, but details will be given later of such operations as may possibly have been concerned in causing the catastrophe.

Briefly then the process was as follows: –

(1) The crude T.N.T. was conveyed by a power driven hoist to the floor of the new structure already referred to, at the top of the building. If the material arrived at the works in barrels these were unheaded by the cooper on the ground floor and the bags were removed and taken to the hoist by two women, but if it came in boxes these were sent up unopened, the screws being removed and the bags taken out by the workers on the top floor.

(2) The T.N.T. was then emptied from the bags into a lead-lined funnel leading into a melting pot under the floor. The melting pot was heated by steam coils two of which contained exhaust steam at about 100°C. and a third steam at a pressure of about 75lb. representing a temperature of 160°C.

(3) The molten T.N.T. was run off through a draw-off a few inches above the bottom of the pot into an open steam heated gutter of iron about 8 inches by 6 inches. This gutter passed over four dissolvers and was fitted with metal plugs which could be lifted to permit the liquid to run into any dissolver as required. These dissolvers were vertical cylinders fitted with stirring apparatus. Prior to running in the molten T.N.T. they were partly filled with alcohol at a temperature of 68°C. After the T.N.T. had been added the mixture was agitated by the stirrers until solution was complete. A partial vacuum was then applied when, as a result of the cooling effect produced, the T.N.T. crystallised out.

(4) The T.N.T. and residual alcohol in the form of a magma or porridge was then run from the dissolvers into centrifugals on a lower staging, where it was whizzed to get rid of the bulk of the alcohol which carried with it the soluble impurities forming the waste product known as T.N.T. oil.

(5) The T.N.T. was then dug out of the centrifugals into bogies with wooden wheels in which it was conveyed along an iron-floored passage to another melting pot, where it was again liquefied

and subjected to a vacuum treatment for further elimination of alcohol. The last traces of solvent were then removed by a current of hot air in a drier.

(6) From this it was run into a pan in which a water-cooled roller slowly revolved in such a way that it picked up a film of T.N.T., which at once solidified on the cold surface, and which was then scraped off by a fixed knife blade to form what is known as 'flake' T.N.T. This was weighed and filled into cotton bags containing 50lb. each, which was then packed into boxes the lids of which were secured with brass screws.

Circumstances Attending the Explosion.

Note:- The positions of the buildings and plant referred to below are shown on attached Plan B [overleaf].

On the evening of the 19th January work appears to have been going on as usual and fortunately the evidence was available at our Inquiry of several witnesses who were actually in the building at the time the fire first broke out, and of two others who had only left it a few minutes before. The shift at work at the time, their hours being 2 to 10 p.m., consisted of 20 persons, 10 men and 10 women.

From the evidence it appears that the distribution of the shift was as follows:-

On the floor above the melt pot	One man (Mauger) and one woman (Lawrence).
At the foot of the hoist	Two women (Sands and Randell).
Packing finished T.N.T.	Five women.
On still room stage	Two women.
Attending centrifugals	Five men.
Attending dissolvers	Two men.
Greaser	One man.
Foreman	One man.

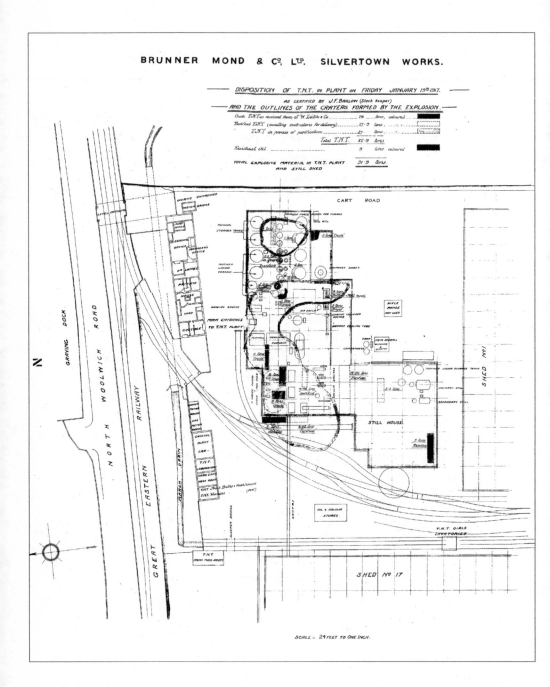

PLAN B.

Immediately before the fire broke out two of the women (Sands and Randell) had gone to the lavatory, and two of the centrifugal men were at tea in the men's mess room.

One of those working on the centrifugal stage was a lad of 17, named James Arnell, who escaped practically uninjured. He states that he was at work sweeping up spilt T.N.T. and alcohol on the evening of the 19th, when looking round to pick up his broom he saw red drops like molten glass falling from the direction of the melt pot room, which was almost directly above him, and the position of which he knew. Apparently Wenborne, the leading hand, who was folding up a tarpaulin on the ground floor, must have seen these drops at the same instant as Arnell did, as Arnell heard him shout to those above to come down. He (Arnell) ran to the main door shouting 'fire'. He then ran through the works, got over the fence separating them from the 'Vanesta' factory, and made his way to the North Woolwich Road. He thought he had been there about three or four minutes when the explosion occurred, and he was knocked down and temporarily blinded. He heard no explosion before the big one.

Hetty Sands states that on the evening in question she was working in company with Ada Randall at the bottom of the hoist, putting crude T.N.T. in bags on to the platform of the hoist and sending it up to the melt pot. About 6.40 she went up to see if more bags were wanted, or if the room was full, and found about 15 or 20 bags up there, Mauger being in the act of removing the last load of three bags when she arrived. The girl Lawrence was cutting the strings of the bags with a small pocket knife, and emptying them into the hopper. There was a certain amount of T.N.T. spilt on the floor, but no heaps, and all was going on quite as usual. So far as she knew the hoist remained up there, where it was secured in position by a catch. On Mauger saying they had enough to go on with she at once rejoined Randell, and they went off together to the women's lavatory on the way to tea. As she passed the clock at the main door she noticed it was 6.45. About two minutes after they entered the lavatory, which was situated about 120 yards towards the river on the far side of the works railway sidings, she heard two faint reports like an iron door being banged. She told Randell to run out and see what it was, and Randell at once came back shouting 'Good God, it is all afire.' On rushing out of the lavatory together they saw the top of the melt pot roof blazing. They then made their way over a sleeper bridge, crossing a large surface drain, where they met another woman, Alice Davies, and reached the corrugated iron fence of the Vanesta Works. While they were considering how they could climb this, the explosion occurred knocking the fence down.

Alice Davies states she was at work in the still room that evening. She had occasion to go and look at the time, and went to the clock near the main entrance for this purpose. It was then 6.48. On returning to the still room which was above the fitter's shop, she had just gone up one flight of stairs when she saw a reflection of fire on another open flight of stairs at the back of the still room. Prior to going to see the time she had heard a noise like the 'shuddering' of a door, but had taken no notice of it. She then ran out and had reached the men's lobby, passing Sands near the sleeper bridge on the way, when the explosion occurred and she was rendered unconscious. On looking back as she ran she saw the roof of the melt pot room alight. She thinks she was the last woman to leave the plant alive.

Frederick Blevins, assistant works chemist, first had his attention attracted by hearing his friend Saunders, who had just left him after a game of draughts in his cubicle, above the T.N.T. laboratory, shouting that the place was on fire. He ran out to the top of the stairs and saw the top of the melt pot room burning fiercely. He went back for his coat and hat and at once ran out, and making his way towards the main gate warned everyone he met to run for their lives. On reaching the time office he turned back to try to find Dr. Angel. He met him near the office apparently on his way from the plant and begged him to run, but he seemed to going to do something at the office – 'telephone or something.' He (Blevins) then ran back through the gate into the road where he warned the firemen that an explosion was imminent, and before he had got far down the road he heard a terrific rumble and was thrown over and over. He is absolutely certain that the fire when he first saw it was at the melt pot and nowhere else.

From the evidence of these witnesses, corroborated as it is by many others, some of whom were able to say that they saw no fire in any other part of the building, it is in our opinion clearly established that the fire originated on the melt pot floor or in the melt pot itself, and that, moreover, it attained considerable dimensions in a very short time. Several witnesses spoke to hearing at least one small explosion before they saw the fire, but it is significant that none of these witnesses were in a position to see the flames until their attention was attracted by these explosions, whereas none of those whose attention was first drawn to the fire seem to have heard any preliminary explosion. The probable explanation of this is that these explosions were merely the kind of occurrence that would naturally result as a consequence of a fierce fire, and would not therefore be noticed by anyone whose attention was fixed on the flames. That the fire preceded these explosions and was not caused by them, seems to us to be clearly proved by the statement of Betts, the chief fireman at the local station, to the effect that he was in his kitchen at the time and heard the sound of a small explosion at the same moment his station fire bells were set ringing. These bells were set ringing by his son whose attention had been called to the fire by a boy in the road. Betts evidence was very clearly given, and we have no reason to doubt the accuracy of it.

As regards the interval that elapsed between the outbreak of the fire and the explosion, a number of concordant statements were made to us, all of which went to show that this was approximately five to six minutes. The lad, Arnell, who was one of the first to see the fire, had time to make his way by a not very direct course to the road, and then to stand watching the fire for three or four minutes. The descriptions given by Blevens, Sands, and others of their movements after the first alarm was raised seem equally to indicate that these would occupy about the time mentioned. So far as can be ascertained the explosion occurred at 6.52; Sands and Randell left the main door of the building at 6.45, and had reached the lavatory, about 120 yards from this door, before they heard the minor explosions. But, as already shown, the fire had started before these explosions occurred, so that it must have broken out very shortly after 6.45.

From the above we consider it clearly established:

(1) That the origin of the catastrophe was a fire.
(2) That this fire broke out in the structure over the melt pot or in the melt pot.
(3) That the fire quickly attained great violence.
(4) That there was an interval of five or six minutes between the outbreak of fire and the explosion.

Quantity of Explosive Involved.

At the time of the explosion the total quantity of T.N.T. on the premises amounted to 83 tons, of which 28 were crude, 27 in process, and 28 finished, and there were, in addition, 9 tons of T.N.T. oil in iron drums, of which 5 tons were subsequently recovered. The Plan B gives the distribution of the explosive throughout the works and the craters formed by the explosion. The outlines of these craters seem to indicate that altogether about 30 tons of T.N.T. and the remaining 4 tons of T.N.T. oil did not explode, but probably burned away. This would leave 53 tons of T.N.T. to take part in the explosion.

Effect of the Explosion.

In view of the exaggerated rumours which have been current as to number of deaths, we have taken particular care to obtain a correct record of all casualties. They were as follows:-

69 persons were killed on the spot, 98 were seriously injured, of whom 4 have since died in hospital, and 328 were slightly injured. In addition we are informed by the police that between 500 and

600 persons who received cuts and bruises were treated in the street or by private practitioners.

Of the 10 men belonging to the shift at work in the T.N.T. house, 9 were killed, the lad, Arnell, being the only survivor, but of the 10 women Lawrence was the only one to lose her life.

The cooper who was also in the building at the time escaped, but his mate was killed.

The material damage was, of course, very great and covered a large area. Everything in the immediate vicinity of the plant was blown to pieces, and projected all over the neighbourhood. Two of the oil tanks belonging to Silvertown Lubricants Limited, were torn open and the oil set on fire, the 'Vanesta' works on the other side were demolished, two flour mills about 350 yards to the north were set on fire by a mass of hot metal, and burnt out, and several streets of small dwelling houses were entirely destroyed, the major- ity of the fatalities taking place here. A gas holder on the further side of the river was destroyed.

It is unnecessary in a report of this nature to give a detailed description of all the damage done, but it is interesting and instruc- tive to note the zones of destructive effect in broad outline. From a survey carried out by the Ministry of Munitions for the purpose of assessment of damage, we are able to state generally that total destruction of brick buildings was confined to an area having a radius of approximately one-eighth of a mile, and most of the fatal- ities occurred within the area represented by this radius, that up to 500 yards houses were partly demolished, and that beyond 650 yards the damage was limited to broken window frames, doors, and ceilings, and was of a character that might be described as slight structural injury. This is, of course, only approximate, and excep- tional cases occurred where the damage was more or less than that corresponding to the above stated distances – much depending on the material and age of the buildings – but these zones of effect are substantially correct, and are sufficient to show generally the area endangering life. It may be noted that in the 'Table of Distances' employed by the Explosives Department of the Home Office as a guide in drafting licences for magazines, the distance considered necessary and sufficient to protect a dwelling house from serious structural damage, *i.e.*, damage likely to endanger life, in respect of a 50-ton magazine is 850 yards, a distance which, in the light of the present explosion, would seem to allow a substantial margin on the right side.

Cause of the Accident

As already stated, there is overwhelming evidence that the fire causing the catastrophe originated in the melt pot room or the melt pot itself, and it is therefore unnecessary in this connection to discuss the conditions obtaining elsewhere. The following description taken in conjunction with the outline Plan C. attached hereto will, we hope, enable a clear impression to be formed of the arrangements in this room, and of the nature of the work carried on there.

The dimensions of this room, which, as already stated, was specially built for the purpose, were 16 feet by 12 feet and 10 feet to the eaves of the corrugated iron roof. The walls were also of corrugated iron on wooden studding, and on two sides there were openings fitted with wooden shutters, but these were always closed at night to screen the light, and were closed on the evening of the 19th. The floor was of stout boards close joined. On the highest point of the roof there was a wooden ventilator of the louvred lantern type. In the south-west corner, about two feet from either wall, was the cage of the hoist, the platform of which, about three feet long by two feet wide, was level with the floor, the open side, secured by a wooden rail, facing north. There is good reason to believe that at the time the fire broke out the hoist was at rest, in which case it could not well have anything to do with the accident, and there is therefore no useful purpose to be served by a detailed description of the mechanism by which it was actuated. In the south-east corner the floor was cut away to admit the staircase, and about 18 inches or so from the east wall was the hopper leading into the melt pot.

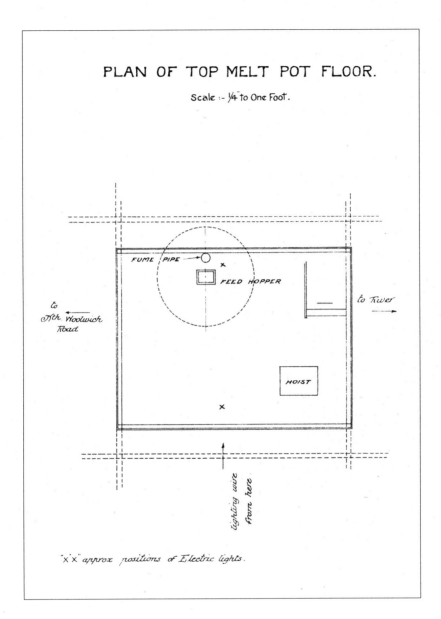

PLAN OF TOP MELT POT FLOOR.

Scale :- ¼" to One Foot.

FUME PIPE

FEED HOPPER

to River

to Nth. Woolwich Road

HOIST

lighting wire from here

"x x" approx positions of Electric lights.

PLAN C.

The melt pot was an iron vessel of a capacity of 5 or 6 tons of T.N.T., and completely enclosed except for a rectangular opening in the cover for the introduction of the T.N.T. This opening was about a foot or 16 inches below the floor level and measured about 16 inches by 12 inches. On the top of the opening, resting on the cover, the lower end of a wooden funnel was kept in position by an angle iron bolted onto the cover, the space between the angle iron and the funnel being packed with asbestos string. The funnel was continued inside the pot to about the depth of 12 inches by an iron section at the lower end of which was a 4-inch mesh grid of half-inch iron rods. The funnel was lead lined, the lead protecting the joint at the floor level and extending just below the joint between the wooden funnel, the cover of the pot and the iron continuation piece. The upper end of the funnel was flush with the floor of the room. The opening in the floor was enclosed on three sides by a wooden hopper about 9 inches high, the front or west side of the hopper being open. Between the back of this hopper and the east wall of this room a 6-inch iron fume pipe from the cover of the pot passed through the floor and up through the roof of the building, a lobster backed cowl being fitted to the top of this pipe. Where it passed through the floor the clearance was made tight with asbestos string so that no dust could fall through on to the top of the pot. It was fitted with an ordinary sliding cast iron damper. As already stated the melt pot was heated by means of steam coils; one of these coils was connected directly to the main steam supply.

A branch pipe carrying the live steam passed through the cover of the pot and led to a vertical coil forming a cylinder of about 22 inches in diameter reaching to the bottom of the pot, where the coil was continued in the form of a flat grid occupying rather more than one half of the bottom area.

There was no reducing valve on this coil, but a small stop valve was provided immediately before it entered the pot, and the steam on leaving the coil was trapped in the usual way.

The maximum boiler pressure was 98lbs., but in the evening it was supposed to have been eased off from 85 to 90lbs. During the day the main steam pipe supplied another part of the plant, but in the evening the T.N.T. building took the full load. The pressure on this coil might therefore been anything from about 75 to 90lbs., and as the tendency of the trap used was to pass steam the surface temperature of the coil must have been somewhere in the neighbourhood of 160° C. Two other similar coils and a grid, occupying the remaining space at the bottom of the pot, carried exhaust steam at a pressure of about 5lbs.

The method of operating the pot was as follows:-

The T.N.T. bags, which had been brought to the melt pot floor, were opened by cutting the strings with a small pocket knife and the contents emptied into the melt pot through the hopper. As the T.N.T. on coming into contact with the coils melted it collected in the liquid form at the bottom of the pot. Under normal conditions of working there might have been anything from one foot to five feet of liquid in the pot. Whatever space remained above the liquid was kept filled with unmelted T.N.T.

A wooden pole was used to push the T.N.T. through the grid and to distribute it over the coils.

The melting point of crude T.N.T. is about 76°C.

Sands' evidence seems clearly to indicate that the only work that should have been in progress in this room at the time the fire broke out would be the opening of the bags of T.N.T. and emptying them into the hopper.

While it has been clearly established that the explosion followed upon an outbreak of fire in or above the melt pot, no direct evidence is available to enable us to determine definitely the originating cause of the fire. Unfortunately the only two workers, Mauger, and the girl Lawrence, who it is supposed witnessed the commencement of the outbreak, have lost their lives. In these circumstances it becomes necessary to examine carefully every possible cause in light of the evidence we have been able to obtain.

For convenience in this examination such causes may be classified as follows:-

I. *Fire of Accidental Origin*

A.— Produced by an outside agency:-
    (a) From a match
    (b) From a spark
        (1) From a chimney or locomotive
        (2) Produced electrically
        (3) Produced by friction or impact
    (c) Excessive heat produced by friction

B.— As a result of spontaneous ignition:-
    (a) Of oily waste
    (b) Of T.N.T.
        (1) As a result of overheating
        (2) As a result of the presence of impurities

II. *Fire produced by a Malicious act.*

I. *Fire of Accidental Origin*
A. *(a) From a match*

No system of searching employees seems to have been established at these works, nor was there any prohibition of pockets in the working clothes such as is usual in explosives factories, but a watchman was stationed at the entrance to the T.N.T. plant whose duty it was to ask each worker for matches before he or she entered the building. The question of searching seems to have been considered, and the conclusion deliberately formed that no system of searching would prevent the introduction of matches or smoking materials, but would merely lead to their concealment in holes and corners in the factory where their presence might give rise to unknown dangers, and it was considered preferable to provide a place near to, but outside the plant, where men could have a smoke after meals or when they had spare time.

This seems to us an admirable arrangement, but it does not altogether take the place of the institution of searching. While we
realise it is impossible to prevent a person wilfully introducing
matches into a forbidden area, searching has a valuable deterrent
effect and helps eliminate the danger due to carelessness in the
matter. We are satisfied, however, that in view of the conditions
which prevailed at these works, smoking on the plant was very
unlikely. The evidence on this point was convincing. Having regard
to what has taken place at other munitions factories, we are glad to
be able to state that smoking among the women employees was
apparently unknown. The evidence we have heard to this effect is
confirmed by a letter received from Mrs. Angel, who for some time
held the position of lady superintendent. Mrs. Angel states that
during the whole time she held this position she never saw a
woman smoking in the factory, and that moreover she had never
seen in the women's mess room or elsewhere any traces of cigarette
ends or of anything that would lead her to suspect that there was
any smoking at all on the part of the women.

In the circumstances we are of opinion that the probability of
the fire being due to a match or smoking are extremely remote.

A. (b) 1.—Spark from a Chimney or Locomotive

In the Schedule of T.N.T. Accidents attached (Appendix II.), three
instances of fire originating from a falling spark are recorded, and
this must be recognised as a source of danger. In the case of the
Silvertown plant there was no chimney in use within 100 yards of
the T.N.T. building, and as the melt pot structure was situated at a
height of about 50 feet above ground level, the danger of a spark
from a passing locomotive can be eliminated. Further, the only two
channels by which a spark could have entered the melt pot room
were through the cowl on the fume pipe, or through the louvres of
the ventilators. The opening of the cowl, however, was always
turned to leeward, and the louvres of the ventilator were perma-
nently so fitted as to keep out the rain, and would certainly not

allow the entry of a spark of sufficient body to light T.N.T., either in the form of dust or vapour.

We feel justified, therefore, in dismissing this possible explanation of the origin of the fire.

A. (b) 2.— *Electric Spark*

The danger to be apprehended from a faulty electrical installation is well recognised, but we have evidence to show that Brunner, Mond & Co.'s officials were fully alive to it, and had taken adequate precautions. All wires were run in steel pipes with screwed joints and outer globes were fitted to the lights. Switches and fuses were outside the building.

During the week preceding the accident the lighting system had been completely overhauled.

The character of the melt pot structure placed as it was at the highest part of the building might have been a source of danger in the case of electrical disturbance of the atmosphere, but the records of the Meteorological Office show that on the 19th of January any such disturbance could only have only have been very slight.

Another possibility to be considered is the discharge between the melt pot and one of the workers of static electricity accumulated in the former, but as the contents of the melt pot were not being agitated, and as the melt pot itself was carried on an iron structure led to earth, this possibility can be safely dismissed.

Taking all these facts into consideration, we are of the opinion that the likelihood of an electric spark having originated the fire is very remote.

A. (b) 3.— *Spark produced by Friction or Impact.*

From the evidence of Dr. Lamb and other witnesses, it is perfectly clear that up to December 29th, 1916, when the factory was visited by Mr. Punter, an official of the Safety of Factories Branch of the Explosives Department of the Ministry of Munitions, the management at Silvertown did not pay sufficient attention to the explosion risk attached to the handling of T.N.T. As a consequence the precautions observed at explosives factories to prevent friction or impact between metal and metal, or other hard substances, and to avoid introduction of grit into the building, were non-existent. Following upon Mr. Punter's visit Dr. Lamb took prompt steps to eliminate glaring evils in this category, and we have evidence to show that on the night before the accident occurred iron tools used by the process hands had been replaced by brass implements. Although this provision had been made, other evidence indicates that the substitution was not complete, and certainly no further steps had been taken to establish what is known technically as a 'clean' area anywhere throughout the plant. In view of this we are of the opinion that a serious danger of sparking – as a result friction or impact – did actually exist. It becomes necessary, therefore, to consider what likelihood there is of a spark produced this way giving rise to a fire.

First, we must distinguish, however, between two types of spark, namely, that produced in the ordinary way between hard substances as, for example, between steel and steel, and that produced by a small local detonation of T.N.T.

Experiments carried out for us by Mr. Dupré have demonstrated the extreme difficulty of igniting T.N.T., and in one case where Mr. Dupré directed sparks produced from a tinder pipe lighter on to the surface of a small quantity of T.N.T. he obtained no ignition until he had heated the T.N.T. to a temperature of 195°C. It is to be expected that more sensitive conditions would prevail in the case of mixtures of inflammable vapours and air, and in this connection we have had the advantage of hearing evidence from Sir Boverton Redwood, who has informed us that, as the result of a very large number of tests made with mixtures of petroleum vapour and air, it was found impossible to obtain an ignition even when showers of incandescent steel filings were projected into the vapour.

In view of these facts it does not seem to us necessary to consider further the possibilities arising out of the production of ordinary sparks of this type, particularly as the condition of the plant at Silvertown was such as to render the production of a small detonation spark more likely, and such a spark would be much more effective in originating fire.

While Sir Boverton Redwood was very emphatic in his view that an ordinary spark was unlikely to bring about a fire, he agreed that the effect of a detonation spark would be very different, and that given the presence of inflammable vapour it would be likely to cause an ignition.

It therefore becomes necessary to consider whether conditions existed which render it possible that a detonation spark was the original cause of the outbreak of fire. As has already been indicated a very short interval of time elapsed before the conflagration had reached serious dimensions, and it would seem, therefore, highly probable that the fire broke out in the immediate neighbourhood of the hopper opening into the top of the melt pot. At this point there are four possible ways in which fire might have resulted:-

By ignition of inflammable vapour
By ignition of T.N.T. dust in the air
By ignition of solid T.N.T. on the floor around the opening of the hopper
By ignition of a thin layer of molten T.N.T. on the iron grid inside the funnel.

Although alcohol was used in the process of crystallisation it is, in our view, very unlikely that any appreciable quantity of its vapour could find its way to the structure above the melt pot, which, as already stated, was right at the top of the building, so that the only inflammable vapour that would have to be considered is any that might arise from the molten T.N.T. in the melt pot. The conditions prevailing in this respect might at times, when the bulk of the T.N.T. was liquid, be very similar the those which obtain above the surface of a liquid undergoing a flash point test by the 'close' method. Mr. Dupré has determined for us the flash point of crude

T.N.T. by the open test, and found it to be 170°C., while that of D.N.T. by the same method is 160°. A 'close' test was not made on account of the risk attendant upon igniting at a high temperature the comparatively large quantity which would have been involved.

According to Sir Boverton Redwood's evidence the flash point by the 'close' test in the case of fairly homogenous substances is not likely to fall appreciably below the open test figure, so that it does not seem likely that a small spark could have ignited any T.N.T. or D.N.T. vapour, which might be given off from the contents of the melt pot. It is possible, however, that other more volatile impurities may have been present in the crude T.N.T.

Again, it has been established that T.N.T. commences to decompose at 120°C., although even at 140°C. the decomposition is very slow. During this decomposition gas is continuously given off, and the possibility of a certain accumulation of inflammable gas in the space above the liquid in the melt pot cannot be altogether dismissed.

We have not been able to ascertain the actual temperature of the molten T.N.T., but from the method of heating and operating the melt pot already described, it is obvious that portions of the T.N.T. must have been subjected to a temperature well over 140°C.

The very rapid development of the fire might be accounted for by the ignition of T.N.T. dust over the hopper, but it seems to us hardly likely that the quantity of such dust present would be sufficient to account for a dust explosion.

As has been stated, a certain amount of T.N.T. was allowed to accumulate on the floor in the neighbourhood of the mouth of the hopper, and a detonation spark from the nails of a worker's boot and grit or metallic foreign bodies in the T.N.T. might have conceivably ignited this material. Any attempt on the part of the workman to extinguish the fire by knocking it out with his cap, as has been done, would probably lead to the projection of burning T.N.T. through the hopper into the melt pot, when a very rapid conflagration would have ensued.

It was the custom when T.N.T. accumulated in the funnel to clear it with a rod of some kind. At one time an iron had been used, but some days before the accident occurred this had been replaced by a wooden pole about 8 or 9 feet long and 1½ inches thick. This pole was also used for distributing the unmelted T.N.T. in the pot and for ascertaining the depth of the molten material. As a result the iron grid at the lower end of the funnel would certainly be splashed with molten or semi-molten T.N.T. Among the impurities found in crude T.N.T., nails are of frequent occurrence and a possibility exists that a nail or some metallic substance introduced in this way was brought by the rod more or less violently into contact with the grid. A small detonation might possibly have been produced in this way. Again, the wooden pole might have picked up grit from resting on the floor above and this grit on the end of the pole striking against the grid might conceivably have produced a small detonation.

In discussing the danger arising from a detonation spark, we have constantly before us the difficulty which is experienced in igniting T.N.T. when an attempt is made to do so, but we have had reported to us (Schedule of T.N.T. Accidents Nos. 4, 5, 6, 7, 8, 9, 10, 11 and 12) several cases in actual practice where there can be no doubt that a spark did ignite T.N.T., either solid or in a semi liquid condition. In view of these occurrences, and in the absence of any direct evidence as to the primary cause of the fire, we are of the opinion that ignition, as the result of a detonation spark caused by friction or impact, must be regarded as one possible explanation of the occurrence.

A. (c).— Excessive Heat Produced by Friction

Cases are known where explosives dust has been ignited as a result of friction from a running belt. The only source of danger of this kind in the melt pot structure was the mechanism actuating the hoist, but we are satisfied from the evidence that at the time of the occurrence the hoist was at rest, and we feel safe in dismissing heating of this kind as a possible cause of the accident.

B. (a).— Spontaneous Ignition of Oily Waste

The danger arising from the spontaneous ignition of oily waste or rags is very well known, but we have ascertained that the management at Silvertown was fully alive to it, and that proper precautions were taken to prevent any accumulation of such material about the buildings. Instructions were issued that all such material was to be placed in an iron receptacle which was kept on the ground floor and was cleaned out daily. We are of opinion, therefore, that this source of danger need not be considered further.

B (b). 1— Spontaneous Ignition of T.N.T. as a Result of Overheating

As has already been stated, it is known that pure T.N.T. commences to decompose at a temperature of 120°C., although this decomposition is very slow even up to a temperature of 140°C. It is quite possible that a moderate quantity of T.N.T. exposed to such temperatures for a very long period would ultimately decompose and spontaneously ignite. It is not very likely that, so far as T.N.T. is concerned, the contents of the melt pot would ever have decomposed sufficiently to produce ignition, as the T.N.T. was constantly being drawn off and renewed. There is, however, the danger that a small quantity of T.N.T. might have found a lodgement on the cover of the melt pot or on some steam pipe, and remained for a considerable period in such a position without being disturbed. One case has been reported to us in which a small quantity of crude T.N.T. which had fallen on to a lagged steam pipe was observed to have burst into flame (Schedule of T.N.T. Accidents, No. 27). In another case (Schedule of T.N.T. Accidents, No. 25) a fire which broke out in a T.N.T. washing house was attributed to a deposit of T.N.T. dust on uncovered steam pipes, and although this might not have been the actual cause, there is no doubt that a spontaneous ignition of T.N.T. had taken place. With regard to the possibility of an unnoticed accumulation of T.N.T. we would point out that in the course of a visit we paid to H.M. Factory, Rainham, where similar operations were being carried on, we found the whole premises in a very dirty condition and with T.N.T. deposited in a great many places all over the plant. In the report made by Mr. Punter as a result of his visit to Silvertown, attention was drawn to the dirty condition of the plant there in respect of spilt T.N.T., &c. It was stated by the officials of the Company that this condition was consequent upon the stoppage for the Christmas holidays, and was unusual, but we are satisfied from the evidence we have obtained, and from the complicated arrangement of the plant, that such a danger did actually exist at Silvertown at the date of the explosion.

B (b).2— *Spontaneous Ignition of T.N.T. as a Result of the Presence of Impurities*

Not much is known about the influence of impurities on the ignition temperature of T.N.T., but investigations recently carried out at the Research Department, Woolwich Arsenal, have shown that certain impurities which may be present in the crude product have a marked lowering effect.

In the course of our investigations, we have learned that ignition can be brought about at a very low temperature, in the presence of caustic soda, and its effect will be more fully discussed when we come to deal with the possibility of malice. In the meantime, it is sufficient to say that the fact that the plant was formerly used for the manufacture of caustic soda and stood in close proximity to the sodium carbonate crystallisation plant of Messrs. Brunner, Mond & Co., raises the question of the accidental contamination of T.N.T. with alkali.

The cooper employed in the building stated that in order to reach his work he passed through one of the crystallising sheds, and he might quite possibly carry into the T.N.T. building small quantities of soda crystals on his boots. While we are satisfied that any alkali which was likely to be about the plant would not be in caustic form, and that the action of carbonated alkali would be very much less severe, the presence of the latter would tend to accelerate the slight decomposition which T.N.T. undergoes on heating.

The normal impurities in crude T.N.T. would also have an effect in assisting decomposition, and in fact a case actually occurred at Silvertown in which a quantity of mother liquor recovered from the crystallisation of T.N.T. dropped onto a lagged steam pipe, and gave rise to spontaneous ignition. (Schedule of T.N.T. Accidents, No. 26.) This mother liquor would consist of alcohol, dissolved T.N.T. and the impurities concentrated from crude T.N.T. On coming into contact with the heated lagging of the steam pipe, the alcohol evaporated off, leaving a small quantity of T.N.T. rich in impurities. This was observed by one of the workmen to burst into a flame, which was described as being 3 to 4 feet high. The explanation that occurred to the officials at the time of the occurrence was that the lagging had been impregnated with alkali when the plant was used for making caustic soda, and steps were taken by re-arranging the steam and mother liquor pipes to prevent a recurrence.

Crude T.N.T. is liable to contain a certain amount of wood and other organic impurities, and we have evidence that pieces of wood and paper were from time to time removed from the surface of the molten T.N.T. in the melt pot. We have been informed that a case occurred in which similar impurities from D.N.T. after being removed were left in contact with a steam jacketed melting pan and spontaneously ignited. (Schedule of T.N.T. Accidents, No. 28.) It has been shown in experiments carried out at the Research Department, Woolwich Arsenal, that organic matter in contact with T.N.T. containing traces of alkali may ignite spontaneously.

Another circumstance to be noted is that, owing to the method of operating, it would frequently happen that a large proportion of the crude T.N.T. in the pot would be unmelted and in contact with the live steam coil, the temperature of which might have been as high as 160°C.

In considering the possibility of the fire having been due to spontaneous ignition of T.N.T. we are again faced with the difficulty that no direct evidence is available. In view, however, of the facts and considerations indicated above, we feel that such an explanation of the origin of the fire must be regarded as a possible one.

II.— *Fire Produced by Malicious Act.*

Careful investigation by police and other authorities has so far failed to discover any direct evidence that this disaster was maliciously caused. The character and antecedents of all the employees at Messrs. Brunner, Mond's factory, at H.M. factory, Rainham, and at Messrs. J.W. Leitch & Co.'s factory at Huddersfield have been gone into, and no suspicion attaches to any one of them. As we have already stated, we are satisfied that it is in the highest degree improbable that any unauthorised person was or could have been upon the premises on the night in question. Nevertheless the possibility that the disaster was in some way due to enemy agency cannot in the circumstances be overlooked. We know that elsewhere, and especially in the United States, the activities of enemy agents have been directed to interference with the munitions supply of the Allies, and we have reliable information that members of certain hostile organisations in the United States have recently been trained by German experts in the art of using high explosives 'for use in the U.S.A. or any other place where they could cripple British interests.' It is obvious that the enemy would be attracted by the project of blowing up a T.N.T. factory situated in a populous part of the East end of London. To achieve this object it is by no means necessary that they should have an agent upon the spot or in the factory itself. It is known that strong alkalis decompose T.N.T. to such an extent that if a stick of caustic soda is introduced into molten T.N.T., even at a temperature as low as 82° C., the liquid in a very few seconds bursts into flame. If, therefore, a stick of caustic soda had been inserted into one of the bags of crude T.N.T., either during operation of packing at the factory of origin or in course of transit to Messrs. Brunner, Mond, it is reasonable to suppose that the contents of the bag would be emptied into the melt pot without the presence of the caustic soda being detected. The contents of the bags were not examined before they were emptied into the hopper, and the result would be that the caustic soda would within a few seconds start a fire which would quickly spread to the whole contents of the melt pot.

We have ascertained that the T.N.T. which was being used on the 19th of January was almost certainly lot 602 or 603, and lot 617 from J.W. Leitch & Co., of Huddersfield. Lots 602 and 603 left Huddersfield by rail on the 9th of December for Dagenham Dock Station, whence they were taken on the 22nd and 23rd December by barge to H.M. factory at Rainham. They were then taken by motor lorry on the 11th and 12th of January to Silvertown. Lot 617 left Huddersfield on the 19th December for Dagenham Dock Station for Rainham, and was sent from Rainham to Silvertown on the 18th of January by motor lorry. Inquiry shows that these lots were mostly packed in barrels and kegs. These barrels and kegs coming from Leitch's often arrived at Rainham with the lids broken in or missing and with the bags of T.N.T. exposed. It will be seen that the journey from Huddersfield to Rainham by rail and barge took many days, and it would have been a matter of no great difficulty for an agent to gain access to one of these bags and insert pieces of caustic soda in it. If no precautions were taken the caustic soda would at once set up chemical action on contact with the T.N.T., but Mr. Dupré, who has carried out experiments for us in this matter, points out that any chemical action of this kind could easily be avoided by some simple expedient as protecting the caustic soda by a coating of shellac, varnish, or even tissue paper, when, in his opinion, it would remain unaltered for a considerable period, and would have no chemical effect upon the crude T.N.T. until it was subjected to the heat of the melt pot.

No doubt some other chemical or some mechanical contrivance might be introduced for a similar purpose.

GENERAL OBSERVATIONS

The circumstances in which it was found necessary in the national interest to establish this plant at Messrs. Brunner, Mond & Company's works at Silvertown have already been given in the opening paragraphs of this report, together with the reasons for continuing its use after other sources of supply had become available.

We fully recognise that in the circumstances the maintenance of output of high explosives is of paramount importance, and that risks must inevitably be taken which could not be justified in times of peace; but from this very point of view, it is obvious that every practicable precaution should be taken in order to prevent an accident occurring which might vitally affect our output.

In the present instance we are of the opinion that certain measures should have been taken by the adoption of which such a disaster might have been avoided, or at least minimised.

In the first place, the arrangements for the adaptation of the plant seem to have been left in the hands of individuals who, although doubtless most efficient in their normal spheres as chemists and engineers, had no previous experience in the manufacture of explosives. It is certainly true that in June 1915, when the conversion of the existing soda plant was first contemplated, very little experience in the manufacture and purification of T.N.T. had been obtained in this country; but as early as the year 1912 the Explosives Department of the Home Office and some of those engaged in its manufacture had accepted the view that the adoption of danger building practice was advisable, and in certain circumstances the precautions associated with such practice had, in fact, been taken.

On July 31st, 1915, the big explosion occurred in the crystallising plant at Ardeer. A Committee was appointed to inquire into the circumstances attending it and one of their recommendations was as follows:-

That having regard to the disastrous and widespread effects of these explosions of T.N.T., the Order in Council dated 11th June 1910, exempting this material from the main provisions of the Explosives Act, should be repealed or amended as soon as practicable, and that in the meantime special steps should be taken to improve the conditions under which it is now manufactured and stored.

The Silvertown plant was not brought into use until September, *i.e.*, after the issue of the report on the Ardeer explosion, but little or no notice seems to have been taken of this recommendation, and the official of the Ministry of Munitions who supervised the conversion of the Silvertown plant had, as he admitted to us in evidence, never seen this report. It is not surprising, therefore, that danger building precautions, even in a modified form, were not adopted at Silvertown.

Again, several reports concerning accidents in T.N.T. factories have also been issued by the Standing Committee appointed by the Minister of Munitions to investigate the cause of explosions in Government and Controlled factories, and in these reports it has been repeatedly recommended that accumulation of explosives in or near buildings where manufacturing operations are in progress should be avoided. It was one of the stipulations under which Messrs. Brunner, Mond & Company undertook the purification of T.N.T., that the stocks of both crude and finished T.N.T. should be kept very small, and these conditions were accepted by the Ministry. It appears, however, that large quantities were allowed to accumulate.

Mr. Mingard, Assistant Director of High Explosives, informed us that at one occasion there were actually on the premises 100 tons of crude and 70 tons of purified T.N.T. We understand that no suggestion was ever made by the Ministry officials as to the provision of separate magazine accommodation.

The existence of magazines would have enabled the amount of material in the working building to have been reduced to the minimum necessary for the process.

It is an axiom of explosives technology that the risk of disaster in a working building is never absent, whereas an accident in connection with the mere storing of explosives is an extremely rare occurrence.

If this consideration had been acted upon at Silvertown, and the bulk of the T.N.T. had been kept in buildings separate from the plant, a disaster of this magnitude might have been avoided.

In the course of our investigations a very unsatisfactory state of affairs has been disclosed regarding the condition in which the packages of T.N.T. arrived at Rainham on their way to Silvertown. In many cases, the heads of barrels and kegs were driven in or missing and the calico bags containing the T.N.T. exposed. In some instances the bags themselves were torn. This condition of things constitutes a serious danger both from the point of view of accident and as affording opportunity for malicious tampering with the T.N.T.

A Safety of Factories Branch has recently been established at the Explosives Department of the Ministry, but it appears to us that, as constituted, the branch has not sufficient power or authority effectively to achieve the object for which it was formed.

Summary of Conclusions

1. The explosion was preceded by a fire, which broke out either in the melt pot or in the room above it.
2. The fire rapidly gained a fierce hold and as the melt pot contained about five tons of T.N.T. in a state of confinement it is probable that the initial detonation took place there.
3. The evidence available is not sufficient to show how the fire was started.
4. For the reasons given in this report all accidental causes presenting any degree of probability may be eliminated, except the two following:-

    (a) A detonation spark produced by friction or impact

    (b) Spontaneous ignition of the T.N.T. in or about the melt pot.

5. Even if neither of these causes was responsible for the fire, the information obtained in the course of this Inquiry and set out in the Schedule of T.N.T. Accidents (Appendix II.) points to the necessity for special precautions being taken to guard against them in future.
6. In the circumstances and for the reasons given in this report the possibility of the disaster having been maliciously caused cannot be disregarded.
7. The magnitude of the disaster was due to the unnecessary quantity of explosive accumulated in the building in which the process was being carried on.
8. The organisation at present existing for the inspection of factories under the control of the Department of Explosives Supply from the point of view of safety and the preservation of output is unsatisfactory.

RECOMMENDATIONS

1. That the Order in Council dated 11th June 1910, exempting T.N.T. from the main provisions of the Explosives Act, should be repealed forthwith.
2. That in circumstances in which the provisions of the Explosives Act do not apply:-
   (a) All operations in connection with the manufacture of T.N.T. entailing the presence of T.N.T. unmixed with acids or water should be carried on under 'danger building' conditions.
   (b) The various processes of manufacture and purification should be carried out as far as practicable in separate buildings.
   (c) The bulk T.N.T. not actually required in process, whether crude or purified, should be kept in magazines situated at such distances from the plant that an explosion in the plant would not be liable to communicate to the magazines.

(d) The quantity of explosive allowed in any one building should be kept at a fixed minimum consistent with efficient working, and a notice should be conspicuously posted in each building stating the quantity allowed.

(e) More care should be exercised in regard to the character of the packages used for the conveyance of T.N.T.

3. That a Department should be constituted at the Ministry of Munitions independent of the Supply Departments, whose duty should be to inspect, from the point of view of safety and the preservation of output, all Government factories and magazines in which explosives of any kind are manufactured, handled and stored.

The inspection reports should be transmitted to the Department concerned, with a view to prompt action being taken on any recommendation made. In the event of the Department considering that it is not possible for reasons affecting output or otherwise to give effect to the recommendations, either wholly or in part, it should submit a full report for the consideration and decision of the Minister.

The Committee desire to place on record their appreciation of the value of the services rendered by the Secretary, whose knowledge of chemistry and practical experience in the manufacture of explosives have been of the greatest assistance to them.

We have the honour to be, Sir
Your Obedient Servants,

ERNLEY BLACKWELL, Chairman
COOPER-KEY.
F.L. NATHAN.
P. TAINSH, *Secretary*
23rd February 1917,
Home Office, Whitehall

APPENDIX I

LIST of WITNESSES in the Order in which they were called

James Herbert Gold, secretary, Brunner, Mond & Co., Ltd.

Dr. Thornton Charles Lamb, works manager, Brunner, Mond & Co., Ltd.

Alfred John Doyle, works foreman, Brunner, Mond & Co., Ltd.

Joseph Hinton, timekeeper, Brunner, Mond & Co., Ltd.

Frederick Blevins, assistant works chemist, Brunner, Mond & Co., Ltd.

James Farmer, leading hand of previous shift.

Alfred James Beckett, foreman engineer, Brunner, Mond & Co., Ltd.

Emma Matilda Farrow, leading hand.

Hettie Sands, worker on melt pot floor.

Susan Fellowes, worker on melt pot floor (previous shift).

Joseph Nattress, worker on melt pot floor (previous shift).

Myra Carston, worker on melt pot floor (previous shift).

Henry Willig, shunter, employed by Brunner, Mond & Co., Ltd.

Henry Blackman, cooper, who opened the barrels of T.N.T.

James Thomas Arnell, worker on the centrifugal floor, sole male survivor of shift.

The Right Hon. Lord Moulton, K.C.B., F.R.S., Director-General of Explosives Supply.

Herbert Albert Humphrey, engineer, Explosives Supply Department, Ministry of Munitions.

Sir Keith William Price, Deputy Director-General, Explosives Supply Department, Ministry of Munitions.

Samuel Scott Betts, in charge of local fire station.

Alice Maud Davies, spirit tester, probably last survivor to leave plant.

Ronald Arthur Punter, B.Sc., chemist, Safety of Factories Branch, Ministry of Munitions.

Robert Crosbie Farmer, D.Sc., Chemical Advisor, Explosives
   Supply Department, Ministry of Munitions.
Herbert Samuel Mingard, Assistant Director of High Explosives.
De Crespigny Brigstocke, T.N.T. sampler.
Major Charles Richardson, G.H.Q., Home Forces.
Lieut.-Col. C.E. Phipps, R.A., C.B, Director, Safety of Factories
   Branch, Ministry of Munitions.
Herbert Smith, Member of Safety of Factories Branch, Ministry of
   Munitions.
William McNab, F.I.C., Consulting Chemist, Ministry of
   Munitions.
Inspector Martin, 'K' Division, Metropolitan Police.
R. Robertson, M.A., D.Sc., F.I.C., Superintending Chemist,
   Research Department, Woolwich Arsenal.
G. Jarmay, technical managing director of Brunner, Mond & Co.,
   Ltd.
Robert Alex. Alston, Director, Explosives Contracts Branch,
   Ministry of Munitions.
Col. William Alfred Churchman, Director, Ammonium Nitrate
   Section, Explosives Supply Department, Ministry of Munitions.
Sir Boverton Redwood, Bart., F.R.S.
John Hugh O'Connor, Manager of T.N.T. Department, H.M.
   Factory, Pembrey.
P.V. Dupré, F.I.C., Chemical Adviser to the Explosives
   Department, Home Office.

Appendix II
SCHEDULE OF T.N.T. ACCIDENTS

Ignition by a spark from a Chimney or Locomotive.

Nature of Accident	Cause
1 Slight fire	T.N.T. oil ignited by falling spark
2 Fire followed by explosion impregnated with T.N.T.	Spark from boiler house on large heap of bags
3 Slight fire containing small percentage of T.N.T.	Spark from locomotive on boxes of rubbish

As a Result of Friction or Impact.

4 Ignition of small quantity of T.N.T. in a drier	2-inch iron flange striking a lead surface
5 Sparking followed by ignition of T.N.T.	Iron screw passing the magnetic separator, and getting onto granite roller of grinder
6 Sparking followed by ignition of T.N.T.	Iron screw passing the magnetic separator, and getting onto granite roller of grinder
7 Ignition of T.N.T.	Breaking crust of T.N.T in steel tray with steel chisel
8 Ignition of Spilled T.N.T. and contents of nitrating pan	Spark from gear wheels carried by slight volatilization of spilled T.N.T. to the contents of the pan
9 Slight local explosion and small fire	Nut and bolt on the washer egg being cut with chisel
10 D.N.T. Oil ignited	Mechanic hammering steam pipe connected to a coil in D.N.T. melting pot
11 Steam kettle (used for extracting dirty T.N.T.) fired	Fired on lifting the lid. This was before the kettle was kept wet
12 Slight detonation and ignition of T.N.T. on side of drier	Additional leverage applied to box spanner by slipping a length of iron pipe along the handle and jerking it
13 Slight detonation	Very gently scraping T.N.T. coated iron pipe with penknife
14 Sparking not followed by ignition	Striking T.N.T. coated iron rod on an iron flange

15	Slight explosion followed by flashing	Nail in boot striking T.N.T. on concrete floor
16	Report and flash in washer	Using spanner with considerable force on flange of run off cock
17	Slight explosion of T.N.T. in mother liquor tank	Nut being unscrewed
18	Slight explosion and smoke	Wooden rod used to clear run off cock. Necessary to use force and rod struck with hammer. After the blow the rod was projected violently from the cock
19	Slight detonation	Nut being unscrewed by spanner
20	Bursting of taps	Being unscrewed for repair
21	Spark and slight detonation	Forcibly opening cast iron cock, rendered stiff by solidified T.N.T.
22	Fire in house of six compartments, in half of which Amatol and T.N.T. were being compressed, and in the remainder gunpowder. General conflagration followed	Ignition of explosive dust as a result of the belt slipping
23	Sparking, crackling noise and smoke in pellet press	Friction of bottom plunger (steel) and the bottom tool (phosphor bronze)
24	Detonation of contents of iron run off pipe on Amatol mixer	Cleaning choked cock with brass rod

Spontaneous Ignition of T.N.T. or Residue.

25	Ignition of T.N.T	Thought to have been due to accumulation of T.N.T. dust on naked heating pipe
26	Ignition of T.N.T residue	Quantity of T.N.T. dropped onto the lagging of an exhaust steam pipe where after evaporation of the spirit the residue ignited
27	Ignition of T.N.T	Crude T.N.T. falling on magnesia lagging of steam pipe
28	Ignition of D.N.T residue	Left in hot pan after ladling out molten D.N.T.
29	Ignition of D.N.T	Molten D.N.T. in contact with hair felt lagging. Spontaneous combustion ensued

LIST OF THOSE KILLED

BIBLIOGRAPHY

INDEX

LIST OF THOSE KILLED

This list of those killed in the Silvertown explosion has been compiled from reports in the Stratford Express. *Where possible, the victim's name, age, occupation and place of burial are given, but in some cases some of these details could not be ascertained from the newspaper reports. Names in brackets represent variant spellings used by the* Stratford Express.

Name	Age (if known)	Occupation	Place of Burial (if known)
Thomas Henry Acton	62		East London Cemy.
Andrea Angel (Angell) Crescent Wharf, Silvertown	40	Chemist at Brunner Monds	East London Cemy.
Henry Badcock	26	Packer	
Sidney Joseph Benstead 26 Lindon Rd, Plaistow	26	Worker at Brunner Monds	East London Cemy.
Ethel Elmer Betts	4mths		West Ham Cemy.
Mary Ann Betts	58		
Ellen Boyce	32		
James Bruce 200 Barking Rd	62	Nightwatchman at Brunner Monds	East London Cemy.
John George Chandler 132 Hermit Rd, Plaistow	27	Worker at Brunner Monds	
Edward Craft			
Frederick Gustav Craft	36		
E. Croft			
Croft, a baby boy	18mths		

Lillian B. Davey	15	Domestic servant	East London Cemy.
John Walter Enness	25	Motor driver at the flour mills	
Edward Forshaw (Foreshaw) 20 Sibley Grove, East Ham	30	Plumber	East London Cemy.
George William Galloway		Engine driver for GER	
Norman Wilfred Gardner (Gardener)	5		East London Cemy.
Edward Godsmark	15		East London Cemy.
William Gray	39	Engine driver at flour mill	
Robert William Greenleaf	17		
Edward George Greenoff 13 Rhea St., North Woolwich	30	Metropolitan Police Officer	East Finchley Cemy.
Alfred Edward Harlow	39	A hawker of oil	
Alexander Hart	25	A checker	East London Cemy.
Charlotte Hiscock	76		East London Cemy.
Charles Hiscock	45	Engineer	East London Cemy.
Catherine Elizabeth Hodge (also called Lizzie Lawrence) 53 Jersey St., Custom House	16	Worker at Brunner Monds	
George Henry Hopkins	24	Worker at Brunner Monds	
John Howard Jubilee Tavern, Silvertown	36	Public House keeper	East London Cemy.
John Royal Howard	21	Bargeman employed by P.L.A.	
Ernest Arthur Jenkins	34	Driller employed by P.L.A.	
Agnes Jennings	23		East London Cemy.
May Gertrude Jennings	20		East London Cemy.
Edward James Kidd 119 Freemasons Rd, Custom House	49	Grain porter at P.L.A.	East London Cemy.
William Lambert 7 York St., Canning Town	34	Worker at Brunner Monds	East London Cemy.
Eliza Lettson			
Henry George Lidbury 40 Hatherley Gdns, East Ham	69	Cashier at grain depot, P.L.A.	
Hugh McCoombs 42 Agate St., Tidal Basin	44	Worker at Brunner Monds	

Hugh McMarsh (McMarth)	24		West Ham Cemy.
Walter Mauger 26 Lindon Rd, Plaistow	26	Worker at Brunner Monds	East London Cemy.
Ellen (Eleanor) Frances Jane Noakes 31 Knights Rd, Silvertown	29	Cook	East London Cemy.
Thomas Oates	8		
Roydon Stanley Patrick	2		West Ham Cemy.
Rosa Patrick	4		West Ham Cemy.
Ruby Patrick	6		West Ham Cemy.
William Patrick	9		West Ham Cemy.
Elizabeth Priscilla Preston 6 Mill Rd, Silvertown	28		
Dorothy Preston	11mths		
George Erick Preston	3½		
Alfred H. Prior	35	Motor driver	
James Henry Reeve 28 Boyd Rd, Custom House	44	Worker at Brunner Monds	
Frederick Robinson			East London Cemy.
Henry Rogers 120 Oriental Rd, Silvertown	23	Worker at Brunner Monds	
Frederick Charles Sell 12 Fort St., Silvertown	45	Fireman	West Ham Cemy.
Winifred Sell (Snell)	15	Scholarship pupil at Central Sec. School	West Ham Cemy.
Ernest Walter (Walter Ernest) Sharp	36	Machinist at Brunner Monds	East London Cemy.
Francis Charles Leonard Simpson 53 Avenons Rd, Canning Town	50	Waterman	East London Cemy.
William Sinden			East London Cemy.
Catherine Smith	16		
Thomas Tasker	53		East London Cemy.
David Earl Taylor Relatives at 45 Boyd Rd, Tidal Basin	69	Nightwatchman at Brunner Monds	West Ham Cemy.
Albert Edward Robert Tyzack	38	Packer	East London Cemy.
Henry Vickers (Vicars) 2 Fort St., Silvertown	49	Sub Officer Fireman	West Ham Cemy.
Sophia Jane Villiers (Villers)			East London Cemy.
Geoffrey (Jeffrey) James Thomas Wainwright	17	Assistant wages clerk	

George Wainwright			East London Cemy.
Elsie Wass	11		
Mary Wass	32		East London Cemy.
Stanley Wass	13		East London Cemy.
George Edgar Oliver Wenborn (Wemborne), 43 Kempton St., Silvertown	49	Worker at Brunner Monds	East London Cemy.

BIBLIOGRAPHY

Garfield, J. *Stories from Silvertown*. Eastside Community Heritage.

McGrath, M. *Silvertown*. Fourth Estate 2002. (Although this is more a family history, it does give an excellent feel for the area.)

Neal, Wendy. *With Disastrous Consequences*. Hisarlik Press 1992.

Paris, Michael. *Silvertown 1917*. Ian Henry Publications 1986.

Ramsey, Winston (ed.). *The East End Then and Now*. After the Battle 1997.

Sainsbury, Frank. *The Silvertown Explosion*. Newham History Society Occasional Papers No. 2, November 1988, pp. 25-44.

Silvertown Explosion archives. Local Studies Library, London Borough of Newham.

Special thanks to Frank Sainsbury, and past and present staff at the Local Studies Library, London Borough of Newham, without whom this book would not have been possible.

INDEX